Student-Centered Literacy Assessment in the 6–12 Classroom

In this practical and accessible book, you'll learn how to create equitable and meaningful assessments in your instruction through an inquiry-based approach. Ruday and Caprino reimagine what asset-based literacy assessments can be and what they look like in practice by understanding that effective, asset-based literacy assessments must center on students: they must incorporate students' unique perspectives, ideas, and experiences in meaningful and relevant ways. Instead of using assessments that focus on identifying what students don't know, the practices presented in this book provide authentic opportunities for students to use what they do know to demonstrate their knowledge of important literacy concepts.

The book is organized into three easy-to-use parts that cover:

♦ Key concepts of asset-based assessment
♦ Specific ways that these practices can be put into action
♦ Putting it all together in your own education context

A great resource for busy teachers, this book features a guide for teachers to use during professional development book studies and ready-to-implement templates when applying the assessment practices described in the book.

Sean Ruday is Associate Professor of English Education at Longwood University, USA.

Katie Caprino is Assistant Professor of Education, PK–12 New Literacies at Elizabethtown College, USA.

Other Eye on Education Books

Available from Routledge
(www.routledge.com/eyeoneducation)

Remote Teaching and Learning in the Middle and High ELA Classroom
Instructional Strategies and Best Practices
Sean Ruday and Jennifer Cassidy

The Middle School Grammar Toolkit, Second Edition
Using Mentor Texts to Teach Standards-Based Language and
Grammar in Grades 6–8
Sean Ruday

Inquiry-Based Literature Instruction in the 6–12 Classroom:
A Hands-on Guide for Deeper Learning
Sean Ruday and Katie Caprino

The Multimedia Writing Toolkit
Helping Students Incorporate Graphics and Videos for
Authentic Purposes, Grades 3–8
Sean Ruday

The Argument Writing Toolkit
Using Mentor Texts in Grades 6–8
Sean Ruday

The Narrative Writing Toolkit
Using Mentor Texts in Grades 3–8
Sean Ruday

The First-Year English Teacher's Guidebook
Strategies for Success
Sean Ruday

Culturally Relevant Teaching in the English Language Arts Classroom
Sean Ruday

What to Look for in Literacy
A Leader's Guide to High Quality Instruction
Angela Peery, Tracey Shiel

Rigor in the Remote Learning Classroom
Instructional Tips and Strategies
Barbara R. Blackburn

Thriving as an Online K-12 Educator
Essential Practices from the Field
Jody Peerless Green

Student-Centered Literacy Assessment in the 6–12 Classroom

An Asset-Based Approach

Sean Ruday and Katie Caprino

Routledge
Taylor & Francis Group

NEW YORK AND LONDON

Cover image: © Getty Images

First published 2023
by Routledge
605 Third Avenue, New York, NY 10158

and by Routledge
4 Park Square, Milton Park, Abingdon, Oxon, OX14 4RN

Routledge is an imprint of the Taylor & Francis Group, an informa business

© 2023 Sean Ruday and Katie Caprino

Library of Congress Cataloging-in-Publication Data
A catalog record for this book has been requested

ISBN: 978-1-032-20725-4 (hbk)
ISBN: 978-1-032-19819-4 (pbk)
ISBN: 978-1-003-26493-4 (ebk)

DOI: 10.4324/9781003264934

Typeset in Palatino
by Apex CoVantage, LLC

Access the Support Material: routledge.com/9781032198194

Contents

Meet the Authors

Sean Ruday is Associate Professor and Program Coordinator of English Education at Longwood University and a former classroom teacher. He began his teaching career at a public school in Brooklyn, NY, and has taught English and language arts at public and private schools in New York, Massachusetts, and Virginia. He holds a BA from Boston College, an MA from New York University, and a PhD from the University of Virginia. He is the founding editor of the *Journal of Literacy Innovation*. Some publications in which his works have appeared are *Issues in Teacher Education, Journal of Teaching Writing, Journal of Language and Literacy Education*, and *Contemporary Issues in Technology and Teacher Education*. Sean frequently writes and presents on innovative ways to improve students' literacy learning. You can follow Sean on Twitter @SeanRuday and visit his website at www.seanruday.weebly.com.

Katie Caprino is Assistant Professor of PK–12 New Literacies at Elizabethtown College. Before her current position, she co-directed the secondary English Education program at the University of Florida and taught middle and high school English at public schools in Virginia and North Carolina. She holds a BA in English from the University of Virginia, an MA in Education from the College of William and Mary, an MA in English from Old Dominion University, and a PhD from the University of North Carolina at Chapel Hill. She also holds her reading specialist and instructional coaching endorsements. Her articles have appeared in *English Education, Writing and Pedagogy, PA Reads, The ALAN Review, The History Teacher*, and *Teaching in Higher Education*. Kathryn is a frequent presenter at state and national conferences and enjoys presenting with undergraduate students. Her professional passions are children's, middle grades, and young adult literature; the teaching of writing; and technology integration in the literacy classroom. You can follow her on Twitter @KCapLiteracy and visit her book blog at katiereviewsbooks.wordpress.com.

Acknowledgments

Sean's Acknowledgments

I would like to thank the wonderful teachers, enthusiastic administrators, and supportive caregivers who welcomed me into their students' educational experiences and made it possible for me to engage students in the projects described in this book. I had an amazing time working with their phenomenal students.

I would also like to thank the students who participated in the projects described in this book. I am grateful to have worked with these talented and dedicated individuals.

I want to thank everyone at Routledge Eye on Education—especially phenomenal editor Karen Adler—for the insight, guidance, and support that makes this organization so exemplary.

I would like to thank my parents, Bob and Joyce Ruday. I am grateful for their encouragement in all aspects of my life.

Finally, I want to thank my wife, Clare Ruday. I can't imagine my life without the happiness she brings to it.

Katie's Acknowledgments

I would like to thank all the future teachers with whom I work. Our discussions give me so many ideas about how to think and write about classroom practices. May this book inspire you to teach and assess your students in meaningful ways that help them grow—and have fun doing so!

I appreciate the support from Routledge Eye on Education, most especially Karen Adler, who has guided us through two books now.

And, most importantly, I thank my parents who inspire me to try to do good each day; Bub, who helps me learn more about literacy each and every day; and Mike, who stands beside me in this wonderfully stellar journey called life.

Support Material

Many of the tools discussed and displayed in this book are also available on the Routledge website as Adobe Acrobat files. Permission has been granted to purchasers of this book to download these tools and print them. You can access these downloads by visiting www.routledge.com/9781032198194. Then click on the tab that says, "Support Material" and select the files. They will begin downloading to your computer.

Part I
Key Background and Context

Introduction

Introduction: Time to Reimagine Literacy Assessment

It's a sunny March afternoon in Virginia and Sean is driving home from spending the day working with a ninth-grade English class. He's not listening to a podcast or to the sports radio station that often plays in his car as he drives. Sean isn't listening to anything at all: instead, he's thinking about his students and the best ways to assess them.

Since he does some of his best thinking while driving, Sean starts to dictate some ideas to his phone. "Assessment shouldn't be focused on what students don't know," he says out loud. "It should focus on what students can do with information and on authentic applications and connections." Sean continues to say, "Students should be assessed in ways that relate to who they are. There should be opportunities for them to bring their assets and unique identities into the assessment projects they create. So much of assessment starts from a deficit model. We need to use an asset-based approach."

For the rest of the drive, Sean thinks about his students, the assets and interests they've shared with him, and ways that the students can show their knowledge of literature, writing, and language in authentic and asset-based ways. After he gets home, Sean takes a piece of paper and makes three columns with the respective headings "literature," "writing," and "language study." Underneath each heading, Sean starts to make some notes about assessment practices that could provide his students with authentic and asset-based opportunities for them to demonstrate their knowledge. Under literature, for example, Sean writes "connections to social issues," knowing

DOI: 10.4324/9781003264934-2

that many of his students have expressed interest in social justice-related current events. Similarly, under writing, Sean writes "community change," reflecting the fact that many of his students have demonstrated interests in bringing about change in their communities. Then, under the literature, writing, and language study headings, Sean writes "multimodal" to indicate his students' interest in multimodal artifacts such as infographics, podcasts, YouTube broadcasts, and other methods of expression. After that, Sean writes "authenticity" under the language study heading, a message to himself to look for authentic applications of the work that students do with grammar and vocabulary. Next, he writes "social action," "memes," and "music," indicating some of the areas of expertise his students have, which relates to corresponding authentic applications of language.

Sean then takes a look at the chart and at some of the student assets he's noted; "And that's just a start," he says to himself, thinking about how his students have many more assets, ideas, and experiences—some of which he's aware of and very likely many others that he doesn't yet know about. "Students need assessments that center them in authentic and meaningful ways," he says.

Centering Our Students Through Asset-Based Literacy Assessment

This description conveys an example of the reflective process associated with asset-based assessment since Sean's reflections, ideas, and subsequent assessment decisions were based on his students' unique ideas, interests, and identities. Asset-based assessment practices create opportunities for students to convey key understandings of literacy concepts in ways that are meaningful to them and align with their funds of knowledge (Gonzalez, Moll, & Amanti, 2005). Teachers who implement these assessment practices decenter themselves while centering their students through opportunities for students to show what they know and can do in authentic and relevant ways. For example, asset-based literature assessment can provide students with opportunities for them to reflect on key issues in a text that are relevant to them and construct multimodal artifacts (such as videos, infographics, presentations, websites, or audio files) through which they apply their understandings of those issues to real-world situations that are important to them. Similarly, asset-based writing instruction assessment could ask students to write about issues related to communities with which they identify while creating opportunities for students to use linguistic forms and structures that are authentic to those communities. In addition, asset-based language instruction can involve students looking for authentic examples of grammatical concepts in their out-of-school lives and conveying those ideas through formats that provide them with opportunities to communicate with real-world audiences through a range of formats. These assessment forms—and others like them—can result in meaningful evaluations of student knowledge that incorporate authentic applications and students' unique perspectives.

In order for our literacy assessments to be asset-based, these assessment practices must be rooted in who our students are. This practice, we feel, is essential for literacy assessment to be inclusive and equitable. Assessments that do not center students by incorporating their unique assets can feel like things that are "done to" students rather than meaningful opportunities for them to express knowledge in relevant and authentic ways. For instance, a student in the ninth-grade class on which Sean reflected in the opening vignette explained,

> Sometimes it's like assessments are just based on things you memorize or if you do things in a really specific way. When [assessments are] like that, they're definitely not relevant. They're just things you have to do the way the teacher wants to get a good grade.

Asset-based assessments avoid this by centering students in evaluation practices and processes. Instead of assessing students solely on factual recall or limited opportunities to express knowledge, these practices are opportunities for students to apply understandings of literacy content in meaningful and relevant ways.

By centering students through our literacy assessments, we can work toward instructional environments that facilitate success for our students—especially those who have traditionally not been well served by our current education system. The 2020 piece "An Asset-Based Approach to Education: What It Is and Why It Matters" published by New York University's Steinhardt School of Education provides key insights into how an asset-based approach to education is important to constructing inclusive and equitable opportunities for students: "It seeks to eliminate deficit thinking and harmful biases that hold back students, especially those with disabilities, English language learners and emergent bilinguals, and students of color" (para. 7). Recently, educators have become increasingly aware of the impact of asset-based teaching and have made corresponding moves to incorporate it into their instruction: "the notion that teaching and learning must acknowledge students' social, linguistic, and cultural assets is becoming more widely accepted today, particularly in urban education" (Woodard, Vaughn, & Machado, 2017, p. 216).

Students need asset-based educational opportunities in all aspects of teaching and learning, such as in the assessment practices with which they engage. Through asset-based assessments that focus on students' individual strengths and attributes, we can move away from the deficit-based approaches described by the previously quoted student. As Valente' Gibson explained in the 2020 National Council of Teachers piece "Working Toward Culturally Responsive Assessment Practices," "We all need to look into our daily traditional assessments and discover ways that we include students and their cultural knowledge, and scaffold their learning with what students already know" (para. 10). By incorporating students' identities and cultural knowledge in literacy assessment in the ways Gibson describes, we can enact assessment practices that create space for them to share their knowledge in meaningful, relevant, and equitable ways.

Why We Decided to Write This Book

We decided to write this book to provide literacy teachers with an instructional resource that will help them understand what asset-based literacy assessment is, why it is important, what it can look like in practice, and how to enact it in their own instruction. The insights, examples, and recommendations we share here build on important insights related to the importance of asset-based education in general (Association of College and Research Libraries, 2018; New York University, 2020) and on recent related work on student-centered and equity-focused assessment, such as Myron Dueck's (2021) *Giving Students a Say: Smarter Assessment Practices to Empower and Engage*, NCTE's (2020) Position Statement "Expanding Formative Assessment for Equity and Agency," and the previously mentioned NCTE blog post "Working Toward Culturally Responsive Assessment Practices" by Valente' Gibson of NCTE's Standing Committee on Literacy Assessment (2020). Our book builds off of these works by providing a comprehensive resource focused specifically on equitable and inclusive literacy assessment that addresses a range of ways for assessment practices to align with students' assets, identities, and experiences. Additionally, this book provides assessment-specific ideas related to important concepts addressed in works about inclusivity, such as Angela Stockman's ideas about teachers centering students and decentering themselves that she shares in *Creating Inclusive Writing Environments in the K-12 Classroom* and the essential insights Jamila Lyiscott presents on student agency in her book *Black Appetite. White Food* (2019).

Instead of using assessments that focus on identifying what students don't know, the practices discussed in this book provide authentic opportunities for students to use what they do know to demonstrate their knowledge of important literacy concepts. By developing understandings of the key features of this assessment approach, its importance to creating equitable, inclusive, and relevant learning experiences, and concrete practices that teachers can utilize when putting this approach into practice, you will be well situated to implement asset-based literacy assessment in strategic ways that align with your students' ideas and experiences. By doing so, you'll be part of an important movement in literacy assessment that challenges deficit-oriented thinking (New York University, 2020) and incorporates students' assets in meaningful ways (Gibson, 2020). Deficit-based English language arts assessments can deprive students of agency and authenticity in their learning; conversely, incorporating asset-based assessments like those discussed in this book can result in culturally sustaining instruction (Gibson, 2020) that recognizes and values the experiences and ideas that our students bring with them to the classroom. This approach sees students in holistic, asset-oriented ways and commits to incorporating those assets into the ways we assess their knowledge.

What to Expect in This Book

We have divided the book into three parts, each of which addresses key information related to asset-based instruction. Part I: Key Background and Context provides essential information that introduces readers to important topics discussed in this book. Part II: Asset-Based Literacy Assessment Practices describes specific ways that these practices can be put into action, describing possible methods of implementation and how those methods align with key principles of asset-based assessment. The chapters in this section discuss asset-based literature, writing, and language instruction, respectively. This information is designed to show readers some concrete ways that asset-based literacy instruction can look in action while also discussing how they can apply these principles to their own classrooms based on their students' unique assets.

Finally, in Part III: Putting It Together, we present closing suggestions for teachers to consider as they put the ideas about asset-based literacy assessment into action in their classes, covering information such as how teachers can make a case for asset-based assessment in their own educational contexts and important suggestions for implementing these ideas. This part also includes resources such as a guide for teachers to use during professional development book studies and templates for use when implementing assessment practices like those described in this book.

Asset-based assessment can reshape our English language arts practices and our students' experiences in important and equitable ways. The student quoted earlier in this chapter on problems and limitations with traditional assessments shared that asset-based assessments were much more relevant and engaging. When reflecting on a language-study assessment in which students identified and analyzed connotation-rich language they used in the social media posts they created in their out-of-school lives, he explained, "I really liked looking for examples of connotations in my life. . . . It was interesting and relatable and much better than taking a test on connotation." Similarly, when referring to a literature assessment in which students reflected on issues of injustice in their communities and compared them to injustices in the book *Dear Martin* by Nic Stone, this student asserted, "This was relevant and interesting. Assessments haven't usually been like that."

Asset-based literacy assessments center students by incorporating their unique perspectives, ideas, and experiences in meaningful ways. To construct learning experiences that truly incorporate who students are, we need to rethink how we assess and focus on evaluation that provides authentic connections to our students' unique identities and cultures. If you're ready to learn more about asset-based literacy assessment, keep reading!

1

Key Principles of Asset-Based Literacy Assessment

How Do I Assess Thee?

One evening early on in the writing of this book, Katie could not sleep. She was thinking of a way to articulate asset-based literacy assessment for herself in a way that made sense. She knew that using multiple assessment modes opened up spaces for students to share what they knew in ways that made sense for them. This idea of thinking about using assessments to help teachers and students see what students *know* was a recurring thought. And then the opening line from the nineteenth-century poet Elizabeth Barrett Browning came to mind: "How do I love thee?/Let me count the ways."

Admittedly, Browning's "Sonnet 43" has absolutely nothing to do with asset-based literacy assessment on its surface. But if we think about the similarities between Browning's speaker articulating the myriad ways she loves the object of her affection and teachers providing students opportunities to share what they know—in the ways that they want to—then all of a sudden, the sonnet becomes a way of articulating the central aim of asset-based literacy assessment. It's not just *one* way Browning's speaker loves thee—it's multiple ways—just as in classrooms that engage in asset-based literacy assessment. And, thus, the assessment version of this poem may open with "How do I assess thee?/Let me count the ways."

In this chapter, we will provide you with the several key principles of asset-based literacy assessment in hopes that you will begin to think about them in the context of your current assessment practices. What follows are

DOI: 10.4324/9781003264934-3

the answers to the following question: What exactly is asset-based literacy assessment?

It is an approach that underscores the idea that assessments should be meaningful—for teachers and students. How you think about the purpose of assessment is critical to the ways in which you design assessment opportunities in your classroom. If you are assessing because you feel you have to assess periodically (we have heard districts require teachers to grade a certain number of writing assignments per quarter, although we are not quite sure why), must give a required district benchmark, need a few more grades for the gradebook, are finished with a particular unit or concept, or are really not sure why you assess students, this is okay. Because even though the NCTE's (2018) "Literacy Assessment: Definitions, Principles, and Practices" suggests "Literacy assessment is meaningful to the learner" (para. 5), we acknowledge that in many instances assessments have become more of procedural requirements for teachers and students. In order to fully embrace asset-based assessment practices, we believe it is necessary for teachers to have a mindset that honors the possibilities that can come when we allow our students to engage in *meaningful* assessment practices through asset-based literacy assessments.

It is an inquiry approach to assessment that is centered on students—and what they know. Instead of thinking about assessments as happening at a particular moment in a unit, we believe that assessment happens all of the time. We are always assessing, most of the time quite informally, to learn more about our students. Students are absolutely central to the idea of asset-based literacy assessment. Knowing students as students but, more importantly, as people is paramount to a classroom that embodies asset-based literacy assessment.

Whereas we acknowledge that high-stakes assessments in the form of standardized assessments may not be going anywhere soon (and even that they could be used in formative ways if students and teachers were not separated by the time the result came in (Wiliam, 2013)), standardized tests are what we are writing about here. As the NCTE's (2020) position statement "Expanding Formative Assessment for Equity and Agency" suggests, "It is teachers, and not test-producing entities or accountability offices, who are best qualified to identify paths that are responsive to the linguistic and cultural resources that students bring to literacy learning" (para. 3). This statement encourages teachers to take on an inquiry stance about assessment:

> An inquiry- and equity-oriented formative assessment stance involves the following dimensions: (1) alignment of purpose, analysis, and use of assessment; (2) a repertoire of assessment practices that suit various purposes; and (3) a broad knowledge base that allows teachers

to align formative assessment practices with larger goals for learning and with student needs.

(para. 7)

Central to this position statement is the student-centered focus of considerations about formative assessment: "Teachers need to be mindful that formative assessment is not about them but about their students" (para. 21). This inquiry approach to assessment permits teachers to engage in assessment practices that privilege students first and foremost.

It is an approach to assessment that honors students' backgrounds and abilities. Related to the student-centered approach shared previously, students' backgrounds and abilities are foregrounded in asset-based literacy assessment. Assessments are designed so as to provide students opportunities to engage in ways that reflect their backgrounds and abilities. Early in her career, Katie taught in a rural community near the ocean. She was intentional in bringing in surfing references because she knew so many of her students spent time at the water. We want to be careful, of course, not to make assumptions about our students' backgrounds, but listening to students and engaging in meaningful conversations with them will allow spaces for their interests to come through.

In addition, as classrooms continue to include myriad ability levels, teachers have an obligation to create assessments in which students with varying abilities can participate. A classroom that features asset-based literacy assessments provides students with different reading, writing, and language skills multiple ways to show their knowledge. At its core, asset-based literacy assessment aligns well with differentiated instruction and the idea of universal design for learning, which considers learners' engagement, representation, and action and expression (CAST, 2018).

It is an approach that is centered on choice. If we think back to the idea of "How can I assess thee/Let me count the ways," we can consider how asset-based literacy assessment allows students opportunities to choose ways they can show teachers what they know. Assessments can still be aligned with standards and require students to demonstrate their learning about particular topics or texts. *How* they do it, however, can be negotiated between teacher and student *or* totally left up to students. Teachers can scaffold this approach to choice in a way that works for their students and their own comfort level.

It is an approach that is grounded in students' literacy practices. Because it opens up opportunities for students to engage in ways that they choose, asset-based literacy assessments often involve students' literacy practices, which may align or not align with traditional school literacy practices. Hall (2010) discusses how students who may appear to struggle with school literacies often engage in multiple literacy practices outside of the classroom. For example, students who appear to not enjoy reading may indeed listen to podcasts or read graphic novels outside of the classroom. Students who appear to not want to engage in writing assignments during class may indeed do a lot of writing (e.g., texting, blogging, etc.) in out-of-school spaces. Asset-based literacy assessments invite students to bridge their out-of-school literacy practices with their in-school literacy practices.

It is an authentic approach. We believe that too often what we ask students to do is not related to what they will be asked to do once they leave the school building. Because they are centered on choice and may engage students in out-of-school literacy practices with which they may be familiar, asset-based literacy assessments can often mirror literacy practices seen in the real world. Whereas an argument can be made for the essay as an authentic genre, it often only has an audience of one: the teacher. However, if students are creating a public service announcement, one of the assessment modes Sean discusses in Chapter 4, their work can be seen by an almost innumerable amount of people. If the goal of our classrooms is to prepare our students to be contributing citizens, why would we not give them opportunities to engage in read-world, authentic assessments?

It is an approach that allows feedback to occur during the assessment process. We appreciate Wiliam's (2013) three-step approach to thinking about assessment. He suggests teachers consider three aspects: "where the learner is right now," "where the learner needs to be," and "how to get there" (p. 16). This approach aligns well with the approach we are sharing here because asset-based assessment allows teachers to offer feedback during the process of completing the asset-based assessment assignments. Unlike traditional assessments, which often are completed solely by the student and then assessed solely by the teacher—with little or no discussion afterward—asset-based literacy assessments allow much feedback at multiple stages. Throughout the completion of an infographic, one of the texts Sean writes about in Chapter 3, teacher and students can engage in discussions that allow learning to occur *during* the assessment. This on-the-spot feedback, the type of feedback we believe maximizes student learning, is generally absent from more traditional assessment modes. As the NCTE (2018) position statement "Literacy Assessment: Definitions, Principles, and Practices" suggests, "Literacy assessments are valid only to the extent that they help students learn" (para. 4). The feedback opportunities as students engage in asset-based literacy assessments ensure that the purpose of assessments stays grounded in helping students learn.

It is an approach to assessment that is constantly adapting. We recognize that students' backgrounds, diversities, out-of-school literacy practices, and available technologies will continue to adapt. Adapting an asset-based literacy assessment approach in your classroom all but necessitates a recognition that how asset-based literacy assessments look in your classroom now will not be the way they look like in the next few years. A student-centered approach that takes into consideration students' backgrounds, diversities, out-of-school literacy practices, and available technologies never could.

Looking Forward

When teachers consider that assessments can become less about what students do not know and more about what students do know, then they are on their way to embracing an asset-based approach to literacy assessment. Now that you have an understanding of what asset-based literacy assessment *is*, we will now discover *why it matters*.

2

Why Should We Adopt an Asset-Based Approach to Literacy Assessment?

As Sean and Katie discussed the purpose for this book, we wanted to be clear about why teachers should adopt an asset-based approach to literacy assessment. After articulating the *what* in Chapter 1, we are now going to move to the *why*. Now that we have a basic understanding of what exactly asset-based assessment is, we want to dig into a question that you, your colleagues, parents, and even your students may have about this way of thinking about assessment in your class.

Although there are several reasons one may adopt this assessment practice, we have honed in on a few answers here. In this chapter, we hope to answer the following: *Why might I adopt an asset-based approach to literacy assessment?*

Asset-based assessment allows for a broader definition of *assessment*. Brown and Knowles (2014) articulated key differences in the definitions of *testing*, *evaluation*, *grading*, and *assessment*: Testing is "a method for determining what someone knows" (p. 209), evaluation is "a judgment of a child's performance" (p. 209), and grading is "a component of evaluation and is an arbitrary label used to place a student along a continuum" (p. 210). We share these authors' ideas about assessment as follows:

> Assessment, however, is a set of strategies for discovering what students know or can do as a result of engaging in learning experiences. It is a comprehensive act that includes consideration of a student's goals for learning, processes of learning, progression toward established

DOI: 10.4324/9781003264934-4

goals, and revision of goals when needed. All assessment should have as its primary purpose the improvement of student learning.

(p. 211)

In this book, we connect with this idea of assessment being tied to student learning. Asset-based assessments allow students to engage in learning as they and their teachers work together to figure out what they know and where they can go from a particular point.

Asset-based assessments provide opportunities for feedback at the most appropriate time. Katie often tells her students the story about the time she "locked" herself in a Barnes and Noble during the first few years of her secondary English career. Her purpose? To grade each of her eleventh-grade students' research papers. Equipped with an array of colored pens, Katie moved efficiently through the papers, offering feedback to her students. Proud of herself for grading her students' papers in one evening, she returned to class on Monday and returned her students' papers. Her smile quickly turned to a frown when a student threw the paper away! Right in the trashcan!

After thinking about what went wrong, Katie figured it out: Her feedback came too late, after students had submitted their work. She changed her feedback process then and there, committing to a writing workshop approach (Atwell, 2015) that provided students on-the-spot feedback they could apply to their rough drafts before submitting the final draft. In many ways, this vignette shares exactly what asset-based assessments provide. They provide opportunities for feedback *during the assessment* that can not only help the teacher know where students may need additional guidance but also help students understand where they need to improve. In many ways, asset-based assessments by their very nature help ensure that feedback will be attended to—not always possible with the other assessment types currently in our secondary English classrooms.

Asset-based assessment may help lessen students' stress and anxieties. In our current teaching context, teachers and students seem especially overwhelmed and stressed. COVID has effected a varying degree of trauma, and we are noticing even with our undergraduate students the idea of taking traditional assessments, especially when for many of them the last year or so has been filled with non-traditional and open-book assessments, causes anxieties we have not seen before. The Pew Research Center (2019) confirmed that even before COVID anxiety and depression were increasing in teenagers. Asset-based assessment, then, allows the temperature to be lowered because it creates an environment that honors students' anxieties. We are not saying that there is *never* room for traditional assessment practices or that students may need additional coping skills to combat the stressors they will, undoubtedly, face in their school lives and beyond, but we are saying that asset-based assessments may help with some of the trends we are seeing in our classrooms and you may be seeing in yours.

Asset-based assessment honors the students' role in the learning and assessment process. The National Council of Teachers of English's [NCTE] (2020) position statement titled "Expanding Formative Assessment for Equity and Agency" suggested,

> The position of this statement is that true formative assessment depends on teachers assuming an inquiry stance, continually asking questions about what learners know and are ready to learn, viewing assessment as intertwined with learning, and practicing accountability with an ethic of care rather than one of consequences. It also requires offering students agency as coinquirers, providing them a variety of ways to demonstrate understanding, and supporting them in reflecting on their own learning.
>
> (para. 1)

Asset-based assessment aligns well with classrooms that are characterized by student voice. In each of the following chapters, Sean discusses various ways to engage students in assessment practices that allow them to question, engage, and inquire. Because of the choices that asset-based assessment offers students, it permits students to be engaged with their learning and assessment in ways that teacher-created assessments with no student engagement do not. Quite simply, asset-based assessment makes students participants in their learning and assessment; as NCTE (2020) suggested "Teachers need to be mindful that formative assessment is not about them but about their students" (para. 21). It's about their future growth: "Assessment provides students and teachers with reliable, useful data about what students know and learn, while also providing feedback so that they can perform even better in the future" (Burke, 2013, p. 295). It is not about teachers' ideas about what students should think or how they should represent their thinking. It is about the students' ideas, and they can help co-construct elements of their assessments.

Asset-based assessment motivates students because it honors their preferences, identities, and cultures. We cannot remember ourselves or our students being extremely motivated for a multiple-choice or essay-based assessment. And this does not mean that they may not have a place at times in particular contexts and classrooms. But we do want to articulate the ways in which we believe asset-based assessments can motivate students. In his text *The English Teacher's Companion*, Burke (2013) wrote, "At its best, assessment celebrates and validates the hard work of students and teachers, both of whom see in the results a confirmation of their own potential" (p. 295). As we allow students to engage in issues that are relevant to their lives (Chapter 3), they are motivated to engage with texts about personally relevant topics. As we allow students to consider changes they want to make in their communities (Chapter 4), they are composing in ways that are meaningful to them so as to effect change. And, as they explore their own inquiries about grammar, vocabulary, and language (Chapter 5), they are exploring self-selected topics in order to learn more. Because it decenters teachers, asset-based assessments can be more motivating for students—and possibly more comfortable for teachers.

Asset-based assessment allows for students at varying abilities to participate in the assessment process in ways that work for them. When we think about assessments, we might think about Brown and Knowles's (2014) ideas of testing, grading, and evaluation, and we may think about those students who are not typically able to engage in the content or assessments without much scaffolding or those students who are typically not challenged by the one-size-fits-all assessment approaches. In the way they allow students to put their own spin on their work and *showcase what they do know in ways they can*, asset-based assessments allow students with diverse academic abilities and preferences to engage in assessments in ways they may not always be able to do.

Asset-based assessment allows teachers and students to meet interdisciplinary standards within a standardized, standards-based curriculum. We imagine there may be some of you thinking that this sounds really super for teachers and students who are not bound by a standardized, standards-based curriculum. And whereas we acknowledge that it may feel this way, we believe firmly that asset-based assessments can work in classrooms that do have to adhere to particular standards—and they may even help you promote interdisciplinary work in more seamless ways. If we think about the ways in which Chapter 4, for example, engages students in considering societal change, we know that literacy standards are being met in the ways in which students are engaging in multimodal composition, but we also know that myriad content areas may be addressed depending on students' interests. For example, if students create a podcast about clean waterways, not only are they working on meeting literacy standards but they are also meeting environmental science standards. We certainly understand that this may not be an easy approach to do when you are an outlier in your district or school. And for this reason, we have dedicated Chapter 6 to how to make a case—to yourself and others—for asset-based assessment practices.

Asset-based assessment practices help students prepare for life beyond our classrooms. Sean and I have yet to be asked to take a multiple-choice or high-stakes test in our personal lives, and we *rarely* have to do formal assessments in our professional lives. We have, however, been required to be reflective professionals and humans. And even though we, as secondary English teachers, may hope that each of our reading texts and writing tasks has a direct connection to students' lives, our students may not always see it this way. Because asset-based assessment practices often include many ways for students to reflect on their learning and their process, we believe that they will be able to develop what the NCTE (2018) position statement "Literacy Assessment: Definitions, Principles, and Practices" referred to as "reflective habits of mind." Students can take these skills, acquired when asked to reflect on their work as part of the assessment practice, into their college classrooms, workplaces, and personal lives. Additionally, as students co-construct the assessment practices with you and their peers, they are working on negotiation and communication skills they will hopefully be able to transfer into contexts beyond our classrooms. Furthermore, the decision-making skills in which students are engaged as they make decisions about the assessment projects in which they are engaged will also be able to transfer.

Conclusion

It is our hope that the *why* ideas in Chapter 2 complemented what you learned about the *what* ideas in Chapter 1. We hope that you are able to articulate for yourself both what asset-based assessment is and why secondary English teachers may engage in this work with their students. The next three chapters will take you through how asset-based assessment can play out in the contexts of literature (Chapter 3), writing (Chapter 4), and grammar, vocabulary, and language (Chapter 5).

Part II

Asset-Based Literacy Assessment Practices

3

Asset-Based Literature Assessment— Moving Away From Quizzes and Toward Authentic Engagement With Relevant Issues

In this chapter, we'll begin our exploration of key practices and methods of asset-based assessment with an in-depth focus on asset-based literature assessment. First, we'll examine essential components of asset-based literature assessment, focusing on its important attributes. Next, we'll consider why asset-based literature assessment is so important to constructing inclusive, equitable, and student-centered learning environments for our students, reflecting on research that conveys the impact of this assessment approach. Then, we'll look at ways that asset-based literature assessment can look in action by checking out specific examples of assessment forms and exploring how and why they represent assessments that align with students' assets. Finally, we'll describe key ideas to keep in mind when putting this assessment approach into action in the English language arts classroom. Our goal for when you finish reading this chapter is for you to know what asset-based literature is, why it's important, and how it can be put into practice. Let's get started by exploring essential aspects of asset-based literature instruction.

DOI: 10.4324/9781003264934-6

What Is Asset-Based Literature Assessment?

Take a minute and reflect on what you think about when you consider the term "literature assessment." Some things that come to mind for us are the literature assessment we encountered as students, such as fact-based assessments like reading quizzes and recall-based tests and formal essays in which students are asked to create and support assertions about a text's theme. In addition, we think about our experiences constructing assessments as English teachers and the ways we've valued relevance, student choice, and opportunities for authentic connections between texts students have read and other works, issues, and students' lives. As we reflect on these issues, we think about the connection between assessment, what we emphasize in our teaching, and what we value as educators. In their book *Bridging English*, Milner, Milner, and Mitchell (2012) comment on this connection: "Thus, we must ensure that our assessments reflect not only what we value about teaching but also what we value about our students" (p. 407).

Since asset-based approaches to education draw on students' experiences, identities, and cultural knowledge (Woodard, Vaughn, & Machado, 2017; Gibson, 2020), Milner, Milner, and Mitchell's (2012) statement about the relationship between assessment, what we educators value about teaching, and what we value about our students is especially significant. When we make decisions about how we assess literature, we're drawing on our values and the importance we place on instructional practices, curricular goals, and our students themselves. When we choose to implement literature assessment practices that incorporate and privilege our students' assets, we're sending an important message that we value who our students are and what they bring to their learning experiences. For example, if we work with students who are engaged in community-related issues and we create assessment opportunities that ask students to connect issues in a text with those taking place in their communities, we are conveying that we value those assets and interests that our students have. Similarly, if our students are interested in working with multimedia, such as sharing ideas through tools such as infographics and podcasts, we can create assessments that draw on those areas of interest and ability. When we make these assessment-related decisions, we can construct activities in which our students can demonstrate their understandings of literature in ways that align with their unique identities, experiences, and assets, thereby incorporating what they've learned about literature with what they already know (Gibson, 2020).

One especially important aspect of asset-based literature instruction is that it is based on the unique assets of our students: it draws from their specific experiences, identities, and positionalities in ways that center them in their assessment experiences. In order for us educators to create assessments that align with our students and their assets, we must learn what our students' assets are and actively work to construct literature assessments that draw on their unique backgrounds, interests, and funds of knowledge (Gonzalez, Moll, & Amanti, 2005). If our assessments do not align with these components, then they won't be truly asset-based. Even if literature assessments are designed with the intention of being engaging for students, those assessments will fall short of centering students in their experiences if they are not based on who students are and the unique assets and experiences they bring to their learning. It's essential, then, that we teachers learn as much as possible about our students' social, cultural, and linguistic assets (Woodard, Vaughn, & Machado, 2017). We can ask students to write "All About Me" pieces in which they describe aspects of their identities and experiences that they're comfortable sharing. In addition, we create opportunities for students to write and talk about their interests and about issues in the world that are important to them. Also, we can talk with students about a variety of modalities through which information can be expressed and encourage them to reflect on modalities that align with the ways they would like to share their knowledge. (In Chapter 7, "Key Recommendations for Implementation," we talk further about ways teachers can learn about their students' assets and implement them into the assessment decisions they make.)

In addition to being aligned in careful and purposeful ways with students' unique assets, it is important that asset-based literature assessment corresponds with the instruction that takes place surrounding a particular work of literature. For an asset-based literature assessment to be as effective as possible, the associated instruction, discussion, and in-class activities should also relate to students' assets, identities, and experiences. If these components are not incorporated throughout the instructional process, there would be a disconnect between the instruction connected to a work of literature and the way it is being assessed. To prepare students for asset-based literature assessments, we recommend introducing the assessment at the beginning of the unit of study and using it to guide all of the instruction, activities, and formative assessments that take place throughout the unit. This will create an assessment-driven instructional process that regularly incorporates students' assets, ideas, and perspectives. For example, if a unit on a particular work of literature culminates with students making connections between the community issues described in that book and issues in students' own communities, the instruction, discussion, and activities throughout the unit should then build toward that assessment and reflect its key concepts. This will prepare students to be successful on the final assessment while also using their assets to help them engage with a text through the unit.

Why Is Asset-Based Literature Assessment Important?

Asset-based literature assessment is an essential aspect of authentic, meaningful, and student-centered work in the English language arts classroom. When we construct assessments about any topic, we're communicating to our students what we most value about their learning. This is particularly relevant to literature assessment and its corresponding instruction because of the many learning goals associated with the teaching and learning of literature (Milner, Milner, & Mitchell, 2012), such as what the assessment (and the instruction that built toward it) focuses on students being able to do and the knowledge from which it draws. Nicole Mirra, in her important 2018 book *Educating for Empathy*, asks a key question about literature instruction: "What *exactly* is it that our students gain from reading and responding to literature that makes the practice so essential to our discipline?" (p. 17).

We believe that Mirra's question is especially significant to consider when deciding how we should instruct and assess students' literature knowledge—and that it highlights the importance of assessing students' understandings of texts in ways that authentically incorporate who our students are. By using literature assessments that draw on students' assets, we privilege the ideas, perspectives, and experiences that they bring to their learning and center students themselves in their educational experiences. To us, an essential aspect of creating a culturally sustaining (Paris, 2012) English language arts class is incorporating assessments that honor who our students are and the unique attributes they bring. Gibson (2020) urges us as culturally responsive educators to learn as much as possible about our students, such as their families, their communities, and the literacy practices in which they engage outside of school. For example, if our students read a literary work—even if it's a piece in which they are actively engaged and to which they make meaningful connections—and are assessed in ways that do not provide authentic opportunities to incorporate their interests, identities, and literacy practices, the students' work with that text will not meaningfully incorporate their assets and work to value and sustain their cultural perspectives. Similarly, if we create opportunities for students to respond to literature in ways that incorporate students' experiences, interests, and skills in both the content of the assessment and the modality in which it is expressed, we will communicate that we value our students in the assessment experience.

All of these asset-based assessment principles create learning and evaluation experiences that avoid harmful deficit perspectives (New York University, 2020). In order to create equitable literature-based instruction and assessment, we need to think about biases that exist in traditional instruction and evaluation practices, such as assessment forms that are designed to benefit students with more familiarity with or exposure to certain texts or forms of language. By incorporating asset-based literature assessments, we can create opportunities for students to demonstrate their knowledge of literature in ways that utilize the strengths they possess. Doing so can avoid deficit-oriented assessments that are embedded with bias. Through asset-based assessment, we can construct inclusive, student-centered, and equity opportunities for students to demonstrate their knowledge of literature.

How Can Asset-Based Literature Assessment Look in Action?

In this section, we'll take a look at three examples of asset-based literature assessments that Sean used with a ninth-grade English class with which he worked. Each description contains key information related to the assessment: the associated text or texts, the product students were asked to create, how this assessment related to students' assets, and what this assessment can show us about asset-based literature assessment. Our goal for sharing these assessment descriptions is to provide concrete examples of what asset-based literature instruction can look like in action in one context. As we discuss further later in this chapter, it's important to note that the best asset-based assessments are based on the particular context and the students being assessed. The assessments presented here show some ways that asset-based literature assessments can look in practice, but the assessments you use with your students will be most effective if they are closely tied to their unique identities, strengths, and literacy practices.

Assessment Example One: *Dear Martin* and Multimodal Social Issue Connections
Associated Text
Dear Martin by Nic Stone (2017)

Product Students Created
Students created multimodal responses in which they identified injustice-related social issues they felt were represented in Nic Stone's novel *Dear Martin* and compared them with real-world events that they believed connected to the same social issues. The students' responses could be shared in a range of multimodal formats, such as infographics, websites, or recorded presentations

that contained audio and visual components. In these assessments, students identified "big picture" social issues in *Dear Martin* connected to the concept of injustice, provided textual evidence to convey how those issues were present in the text, and analyzed what the textual evidence communicated to readers about that topic. For example, if a student selected the issue of racial profiling, a key concept in the novel, they would identify that topic, share excerpts from the text that illustrate its role in the book, and then analyze how those passages represent and relate to this idea. After sharing that information and the corresponding insights, students described real-world situations from current events or from history, finding information from credible sources related to that topic. Once they identified this material, the students analyzed ways that the real-life events and the relevant events in *Dear Martin* related to each other. Since the essential question for the class's study of the novel was "How do people act in the face of injustice and what does that say about them?", the students were expected to incorporate the idea of responding to injustice in their identifications and analyses of issues and excerpts from *Dear Martin* as well as their research and analysis related to real-world events.

How This Assessment Related to Students' Assets

The students in the ninth-grade class with which Sean worked demonstrated great interest and proficiency regarding social justice-related issues in the world and the creation of multimodal artifacts. Sean recognized these assets the students possessed and use them to inform this assessment. The multimodal artifacts the students created incorporated their insights about social-justice issues represented in *Dear Martin* and real-world events that represent similar issues. This assessment centered students' assets in the response's modality, the aspect of the text on which their analyses focused, and the kinds of connections to the text they created. The students' assets were central to the construction of this unit of study from its beginning: before the class began reading *Dear Martin*, Sean thought about the students' engagement and familiarity with multimodal texts and social issues and used that information to construct the unit's assessment, essential question, and daily lessons. By reflecting on these assets and thinking about effective ways to incorporate them into the students' work with this text and the assessment of their knowledge of it, Sean was able to create an assessment that centered students and provided them with a way to demonstrate their knowledge that was relevant to their interests, identities, and experiences.

What This Assessment Can Show Us About Asset-Based Literature Assessment

This assessment provides an example of how literature assessment can combine in-depth analysis with opportunities for students to authentically incorporate their assets. In this assessment, students completed a range of analyses: they explored how the excerpts from *Dear Martin* they identified reflected a social issue described in the book and discussed connections between what took place in the text and a real-world issue they identified. In addition to incorporating these analytical components, this assessment drew on a number of student assets and interests: the students' interests in social justice-related issues in the world and their engagement with multimodal forms. This assessment conveys that asset-based literature assessment can incorporate a range of forms of in-depth analysis, can incorporate topics and issues that students value, and can be delivered in modalities that align with students' authentic assets and forms of communication. Asset-based educational practices, like the literature assessment described here, will certainly vary based on specific context; this discussion provides one example of an asset-based assessment that is informed by students' unique attributes, the text, and the instructional goals associated with it.

Assessment Example Two: *Piecing Me Together*, Goals, and Podcasts
Associated Text
Piecing Me Together by Renée Watson (2017)

Product Students Created
In this assessment, students created podcasts in which they discussed a goal they would like to achieve, how they plan to achieve that goal, and how achieving that goal would help them make a positive impact on the world. In their podcasts, students were required to interview a guest that they felt could share expertise on the goal and how achieving it could help them impact the world in a positive way. In addition, students used a portion of their podcast to compare the goal they want to achieve and the impact it can have on society with the experiences of Jade, the main character of *Piecing Me Together*. In these analyses, students focused on analysis-oriented information, such as what Jade's goals show us about her and what each student's goals and the impact of those goals convey about their values and interests. Students also created websites that introduced their podcasts. In these websites, students discussed the key content of their podcasts, described the person they interviewed, and provided any other information they thought would be useful to the listener's understanding of the podcast. The essential question for the class's study of *Piecing Me Together* was "What is the role of goal-setting in life?" This assessment provided the students with an asset-based opportunity to examine issues related to that question and the issues discussed in the text.

How This Assessment Related to Students' Assets

As Sean continued to teach and interact with the ninth-grade English class with which he worked, he learned that another important attribute the students in the class possessed was their interest in talking about their future goals. During class discussions as well as unstructured times, students frequently made connections to goals they had. These goals represented a variety of types and topics: some were career goals, while others represented more immediate actions they would like to take, such as leading a demonstration in the community to generate awareness of an issue or raising money for a local family who had been significantly impacted by the pandemic. In addition, Sean learned that the students frequently listened to podcasts related to their interests and enjoyed recommending high-interest podcasts to each other.

Once he learned about students' interests in goal-setting and podcasts, Sean looked for ways to connect this asset the students possessed with other assets he had already noted: their interest in social issues and their skill and experience with a range of multimodal responses. This assessment combines these assets by incorporating students' interests in goal setting, social issues, multimedia responses, and podcasts. To prepare students for this assessment, Sean brought in examples of podcasts for the class to discuss and encouraged students to share podcasts they enjoyed. The students analyzed the podcasts as mentor texts, noting the strategies hosts used to introduce topics, conduct interviews, and share concluding insights. This combination of topics and modalities resulted in an assessment that was specific to students' assets and interests.

What This Assessment Can Show Us About Asset-Based Literature Assessment

An especially important aspect of this assessment is the way it was informed by Sean's continued experience learning about his students' assets. He had already developed an awareness of interests and assets his students possessed, such as their engagement with social-justice issues and multimedia texts, and used that information to inform previous assessments (such as the assessment on *Dear Martin* described earlier in this chapter). However, as Sean continued to interact with his students, he learned about their passion for discussing a range of future goals and their interest in listening to and discussing podcasts. Sean saw these attributes as important assets that could be used to make his students' literacy assessment as student-centered, meaningful, and asset-based as possible.

Sean's experience learning more about his students' assets and using this information to craft an asset-based literature assessment on *Piecing Me Together* has important applications for other educators as they created asset-based assessment for their students: it shows that the process of learning about students' assets is an ongoing and fluid journey. We might know some of our students' assets early in the school year, but it is important that we keep listening and learning to find out more about our students' experiences, interests, and identities. It is very possible that our students develop new and/or different interests throughout the school year and there is certainly more that we can learn about our students than what we know early on in the year. As we educators continue to listen to and learn from our students, we can create additional ways for students to draw on their assets and demonstrate their knowledge in authentic and meaningful ways.

Assessment Example Three: Independent Reading, Justice, and Community Event Proposals

Associated Text

In this unit, students selected independent reading books. The only requirement was that the books addressed issues of justice and/or injustice in some way to align with the unit's essential question "What does it mean to work for justice?"

Product Students Created

In this assessment, students created proposals for community events. These proposed events were connected to a justice-oriented issue discussed in the book they read. For example, if a student read a book that addressed a particular form of discrimination or unequal treatment, they might then create a proposal for an event in the community that raised awareness of that issue. (For instance, if a student read *The Hate U Give* by Angie Thomas (2017), they might propose an event designed to increase awareness of and challenge the systemic racism discussed in the novel.) An event proposal could also be modeled on the justice-oriented work in a text: such as, if a character in a book worked for justice in a particular way, a student could create a proposal for a community event that was inspired by that character's work for justice. (One illustration of this is that a student who read *The Epic Fail of Arturo Zamora* by Pablo Cartaya might propose an event designed to preserve small and family-owned businesses that reflect a community's cultural heritage, as protagonist Arturo does in this book.)

Students created written proposals as well as visual presentations. In the written proposals, students described the event they were proposing by first providing an overview of the event and then discussing the justice-oriented issue it addresses, why that issue is especially significant, and how it addresses that issue. After that, students went into the connections between the issue the event addresses and their independent reading book, highlighting the ways the issue is present in the book they read and how the event and the book can both raise awareness of the issue. Finally, the students discussed specific details of their proposed events, such as potential budgets, community stakeholders to whom they might reach out, a possible location, and specific ways they would generate publicity for the event. The presentations contained highlights from these written reports and were given in the school's auditorium to classmates, other students in the school, and family and community members that students chose to invite. Both the written proposals and the visual presentations were designed to incorporate multimedia: in both pieces, students incorporated images of the potential venue for the event, multimedia connections to ways they would generate publicity, visuals associated with community stakeholders, and charts and graphs used to convey the features of their budgets. Students also had the option of incorporating multimedia associated with the justice-oriented issue discussed in their proposal to further inform readers of information associated with it.

How This Assessment Related to Students' Assets

This assessment incorporated the students' interests in social issues and multimodality and combined those assets with the students' engagement with their communities and the desire that many demonstrated in making change in their communities. In class discussions throughout the year, students skillfully made connections to important issues and events taking place in communities in which they were a part. (In this case, "community" has a wide-ranging meaning: some students made connections to the town where they lived while others identified other communities to which they belonged, such as affinity groups, cultural identities, athletic and artistic activities, and other forms.) In addition, this project in general related to students' strong interest in reading books of their own choice by incorporating their independent reading texts as a key part of their literature instruction and assessment.

This assessment was designed to create space for students to draw on their interests in and assets related to social issues, multimodal expression, and community-related topics. Sean's goal in constructing it was to provide an authentic opportunity for students to share their insights related to these topics in ways that were informed by their experiences with and understandings of their independent reading books. He sought to construct an opportunity for students to be centered in their assessment experiences through a range of choices and flexibility (such as the text the students identified, the corresponding issue they noticed in it, the type of event they would like to plan, and the ways they would go about constructing that event) while still providing sufficient structure to help students navigate a challenging and multi-step process.

What This Assessment Can Show Us About Asset-Based Literature Assessment

One especially significant aspect of this assessment is that it conveys how asset-based literature assessment naturally lends itself to authentic applications of knowledge. Since the students in Sean's class demonstrated engagement in their communities and in social justice-related concepts, it followed logically that an asset-based assessment would incorporate these components in ways that provided students with opportunities to apply their knowledge in ways that connected to the world around them. While this is one specific example of an authentic and asset-based assessment that was directly connected to the features of its particular context (such as the types of books students selected, the class's essential question, and the students' interests in social issues, community, and multimodality), the idea of providing students with authentic applications of their knowledge can be incorporated into a range of asset-based assessments. As you construct asset-based literature assessments for your students, we encourage you to create space for your students to apply their ideas to real-world situations. For example, students can make real-world connections to texts, write letters to relevant stakeholders, create websites and social media accounts meant to raise awareness of a topic, craft proposals for community events, or put together other relevant products. The most important aspect of such an assessment is that it is authentically aligned with students' assets and interests: this alignment is what will center our students in their assessment experiences and provide them with meaningful opportunities to show their knowledge in ways that incorporate their experiences and identities.

Key Ideas to Keep in Mind When Putting Asset-Based Literature Assessment Into Action

In this section, we present five ideas to consider when incorporating asset-based literature assessments in your classrooms. These insights will help you maximize the effectiveness of your assessments by linking them closely with students' assets. The five points we recommend keeping in mind are:

- ◆ Begin by reflecting on your literature assessment experiences.
- ◆ Consider the role of literature assessment: what has it been and what can it be?
- ◆ Build relationships with your students.
- ◆ Learn about your students' assets.
- ◆ Incorporate your students' assets into their literature assessments, while continuing to make space for additional understandings.

Now, let's take a look at each of these specific insights.

Begin by Reflecting on Your Literature Assessment Experiences

To start the journey of moving toward (or further implementing) asset-based literature assessment in your classroom, we recommend reflecting on your experiences with literature assessment as both a student and as a teacher. By considering these ideas, you'll start the process of thinking about what you've most noticed about literature assessment and activate your prior knowledge about this topic in ways that will help prepare you to further reflect on the benefits of asset-based literature assessment and ultimately implement it into your instruction. For example, when reflecting on your experiences as a student, you can ask yourself questions such as:

- ◆ How was my knowledge of literature typically assessed?
- ◆ What do I remember about these assessments?
- ◆ What did I do when I prepared for these assessments?

Similarly, we recommend reflecting on the literature assessments you have incorporated in your classroom and considering what has most stood out to you about those opportunities for students to express their knowledge. When doing so, you might reflect on questions like:

- ◆ What are some ways I have assessed my students' knowledge of literature?
- ◆ Which literature assessments seem to have best motivated my students to learn and express their knowledge?
- ◆ Why do I think those assessments were especially effective?

Note: These questions are also available in an easily-reproducible format in Appendix B.

These questions will guide your thinking about your insights and perspectives regarding literature assessment and will position you to continue to think about and reflect on ideas related to asset-based assessment discussed in this process.

Consider the Role of Literature Assessment: What Has It Been and What Can It Be?

Once you have reflected on your experiences with literature assessment as both a student and a teacher, we recommend thinking about the role that literature assessment has played in the English language arts classroom as well as the possibilities that are embedded in it. In her essential 2015 book *Culturally Relevant Teaching & the Brain*, Zaretta Hammond calls attention to deficit-oriented assessment and instruction practices that focus primarily on factual recall and do not provide students with authentic opportunities to use knowledge in meaningful ways. Hammond explains that these deficit-oriented practices contribute to educational inequities and are used especially frequently with "culturally and linguistically diverse students" (p. 5). Urging educators to be aware of students' cultures and assets, Hammond asserts "When we are able to recognize and name a student's learning moves and not mistake culturally different ways of learning and making meaning for intellectual deficits, we are better able to match those moves with a powerful teaching response" (p. 5).

Hammond's insights have important relevance to asset-based literature assessment. Instead of focusing on student recall of factual events and quotations from texts as literature assessment sometimes does (Milner, Milner, & Mitchell, 2012), we can implement assessment practices that align with students' assets, identities, and ways of learning—in Hammond's words, we can center our students' "learning moves" and "culturally different ways of learning" (p. 5). By centering these important aspects and attributes, we can incorporate literature assessments like the ones described in the chapter that provide students with authentic and student-centered opportunities to demonstrate their knowledge of literature in meaningful ways. For example, we can construct assessments that incorporate ways for students to apply their understandings of literary texts to interests and assets they have, such as the world around them, multimodal forms of expression, community issues, or any other assets that are unique and specific to them. These assessment practices can help us educators construct meaningful and relevant opportunities for students to convey their knowledge.

Build Relationships With Your Students

An essential aspect of creating and implementing literature assessment practices that center your students is building relationships with them that help them feel comfortable in the classroom. Through these relationships, teachers can build authentic connections with students that help them learn about their students as learners, thinkers, as people. In the article "Cultivating a Culturally Responsive Classroom Community," Jocelyn Stephens (2017) describes important practices for teachers to implement when building relationships with students, explaining that teachers should: share stories about their lives and create opportunities for students to share stories about themselves, listen actively, show students through their actions that they care about them, and communicate to students that they want to get to know their students individually. Through these practices, you can create strong relationships with your students and build supportive classroom communities in which your students feel comfortable as learners and as people. By constructing these relationships and a corresponding supportive community, you will create a learning environment in which students feel centered and valued.

Learn About Your Students' Assets

Once you've constructed a supportive learning environment and worked to build strong relationships with students, you'll be well positioned to listen to and learn about your students' assets, identities, and experiences. There are countless forms students' assets can take, such as family and community funds of knowledge (Gonzalez, Moll, & Amanti, 2005), experiences, interests, forms of technology with they are comfortable and familiar, modalities of texts with which they frequently interact (such as infographics, podcasts, TED talks, and others), and many more. The most important aspect of this process is to take a listening role and grow to understand the assets which our students bring to the classroom. As you engage in this listening and learning process, it's important to keep in mind that the role of the teacher in this situation is to create a safe space for students to share their assets, identities, and experiences. Some students will share more of this information than others and some classes in general will feel more comfortable sharing these assets. By building relationships and creating a supportive classroom community, you will have constructed a situation in which students can share what matters to them and the ways in which they engage with the world. As Sean learned about his students in preparation for the literature assessments described in this chapter, he wrote down assets he noticed and ways the students displayed them. Appendix B contains a reproducible document titled "Notes on Students' Assets" that you can use when recording students' assets that you've identified while working with them.

As you learn about students' assets, it's important to note that it's likely that there will be differences in your students' experiences, interests, and identities as well as some similarities. When noting his students' assets, Sean looked for key similarities that existed and could then be applied in a variety of ways. For example, regarding the third assessment example described in this chapter, there were a great deal of differences in the types of communities with which students identified and the specific issues students felt were important. However, the idea of community engagement was something that students valued and appreciated opportunities to discuss. With this in mind, Sean constructed an assessment that addressed the idea of community events while doing so in a way that provided a range of opportunities for students to approach the project in forms that aligned with their interests and assets.

Incorporate Your Students' Assets Into Their Literature Assessments, While Continuing to Make Space for Additional Understandings

Once you've completed all of the preceding aspects of this process, such as reflecting on your experiences with literature assessment, thinking about its role in the curriculum, building relationships with your students, and learning about their assets, you'll be perfectly prepared for the final component: incorporating your students' assets into their literature assessments. As the examples in this chapter illustrate, students can have a range of assets, experiences, and interests that can be incorporated into their literature assessments. These assets can relate to the content students address in their assessments (such as identifying social justice-related issues in a book with real-world events as discussed in the first assessment example) and can also relate to the modality students use to express their understandings (like the podcasts students created in the second assessment example). By valuing these different types of assets, interests, and experiences, we educators can further convey to students how much we appreciate who they are as individuals. When we are aware of the many possible assets our students bring to the classroom and work to implement them into literature assessment, we send a message to students that their work with literature assessment is about *them*: their interests, assets, identities, and positionalities. This practice communicates to students that assessment is not solely about recalling information from a text; instead, it's about demonstrating their knowledge in relevant and meaningful ways that align with who our students are. The document in Appendix B titled "Asset-Based Literature Assessment Planning Guide" is an excellent resource for considering how you'll incorporate asset-based literature assessment with your students; this planning guide asks you to identify the student asset that is central to the assessment, the literary text or texts on which students are demonstrating their knowledge, what students will be asked to do in the assessment, how the assessment aligns with students' assets, and how it will allow students to display their knowledge of the text.

One important thing to note about asset-based literature assessment is that, as teachers, our knowledge of students' assets is fluid and continuous. Our students' assets and interests may change throughout the school year and our knowledge of our students will also develop over time. For example, the second assessment example described in this chapter was informed by Sean's continued understanding of his students. As he continued to learn more about his students and their interests in discussing their future goals, he used this knowledge to inform the assessments that he created for the students. When you work to create asset-based literature assessments with your students, we encourage you to approach this endeavor with the understanding that you will continue to learn more about your students' ideas, interests, and perspectives as the school year goes on: as you learn this information, you can then incorporate it in ways that provide students with asset-based and student-centered opportunities to convey their knowledge.

4

Asset-Based Writing Assessment—Exploring Societal Change, Multimodal Expression, and Linguistic Diversity

Now that we've explored asset-based literature assessment, we'll examine in this chapter what it looks like to apply an asset-based approach to writing assessment. To begin, we'll describe what asset-based writing assessment is, highlighting especially significant components of this approach. After that, we'll discuss why asset-based writing assessment is important; to do so, we'll share insights and relevant research that illustrates how this approach centers students, promotes inclusivity, and emphasizes equity in the literacy classroom. Next, we'll check out specific ways that asset-based writing assessment can look in practice by taking a look at some examples of assessments Sean used with his ninth graders. In addition to sharing descriptions of these assessment examples, we'll also discuss how the assessments aligned with students' assets and what they show about asset-based writing assessment. We'll then conclude the chapter with key ideas to keep in mind when incorporating asset-based writing assessment in your English language arts classroom. As we'll describe in this chapter, asset-based writing assessment is an essential aspect of an inclusive and student-centered learning environment. Let's begin our exploration of this important topic by considering key aspects of this approach!

DOI: 10.4324/9781003264934-7

What Is Asset-Based Writing Assessment?

In order for us as educators to purposefully and meaningfully incorporate students' assets into our curricula, we need to think carefully about writing assessment. When Sean began considering the best ways to utilize asset-based writing assessment with the ninth graders he taught, he reflected on his students' assets, interests, and identities, noting their passion for inspiring community change, their interest in multimodal expression, and the many different forms of language they use. With these ideas in mind, Sean sought to create opportunities for his students to write in ways that aligned with their particular assets, constructing ways for them to show their knowledge of key writing strategies, concepts, and standards that related to their unique identities. Because of the unique positionalities of his students, Sean constructed assessments that incorporated issues of societal change, uses of multimodal expression, and opportunities for linguistic diversity.

It's important to note that asset-based writing assessment needs to be purposefully aligned with who our students are as writers. To do this, we can consider concepts such as the topics about which students are passionate, the modalities they use, the audiences with whom they would like to connect, the cultural and linguistic experiences that have informed their uses of language, and much more. Because of this, it's essential that we teachers get to know our students as writers, thinkers, communicators, and, most importantly, people: then, we can use that knowledge to construct opportunities for students to demonstrate their writing expertise in authentic and relevant ways. For instance, if our students have passion for or experience with visual art or photography, we can create opportunities for our students to utilize those assets while demonstrating their knowledge as writers. Sean once worked with a student who was very creative and gifted with drawing, but had difficulty expressing his ideas in writing; as he and this young man worked together, the student continued to create his creative drawings and Sean helped him make connections between those visual artworks and written expression. Similarly, students whose understandings of literacy are informed by stories told in their communities shouldn't be told that those community stories are separate from the writing they do in school. Instead, they can use those experiences and assets with community literacy experiences to show their knowledge of what effective writing is and why.

Katie Van Sluys (2011) thoughtfully described the flexibility embedded in effective writing assessment: "Assessment is flexible and designed to capture, and help teachers and students understand and act on, the rich information embedded in the diverse language experiences that young people bring with them into classrooms" (pp. 94–95). One aspect of this discussion of effective writing assessment that is particularly relevant to the ideas described in this chapter (and in this book as a whole) is the way it privileges the language experiences that students have outside of school and advocates centering those experiences in the writing assessment that takes place in school. While asset-based writing assessment will look different with different students based on their unique experiences and positionalities, some aspects will be consistent: this type of assessment creates space for students to utilize the communication forms, styles, and modalities that they bring into the classroom and draws on their unique funds of knowledge (Gonzalez, Moll, & Amanti, 2005). Asset-based writing assessment constructs opportunities for our students to convey their knowledge of writing in school while drawing on the forms and methods of communication that are authentic to them.

Why Is Asset-Based Writing Assessment Important?

Asset-based writing assessment is essential to creating student-centered and inclusive writing environments that facilitate students' abilities to be successful and to learn in culturally sustaining (Paris, 2012) contexts. As we've previously discussed, asset-based approaches to education draw on students' identities, experiences, and cultures (Woodard, Vaughn, & Machado, 2017) and seek to eliminate biases and deficit thinking (New York University, 2020). These points are especially relevant to reflections on and conversations about writing assessment, given what it has often valued: traditionally, writing assessment has frequently limited the modalities students can use to share their ideas (Stockman, 2020), focused on specific, teacher-selected topics (Robb, 2010), emphasized White Mainstream English (Baker-Bell, 2020), and called for students to write for limited and often inauthentic audiences (Fletcher & Portalupi, 2001). In contrast, writing assessment that draws on students' assets holds space for our students to write and communicate in ways that are meaningful to them and incorporate the experiences, identities, and insights they bring to the classroom. By doing this, we educators can construct situations in which opportunities for success are more equitably distributed than they would be in traditional writing assessment that focuses on specific genres, topics, audiences, and forms of language. Writing assessments that purposefully incorporate students' assets and provide them with opportunities to draw on those assets while meeting curricular standards increase the opportunities for success for our students.

Another important benefit of asset-based writing assessment is that it helps students write in ways that align with real-world applications of writing skills and strategies. Since our students' writing assets and interests are rooted in their authentic experiences, incorporating those assets into our assessment (and into the corresponding instruction aligned with that assessment) provides students with opportunities to write in ways that not only interest them but also are reflective of real-world communication strategies. For example, if we look at some authentic examples of writing, such as articles in magazines and on websites, we can see that those pieces employ tactics that may be aligned with students' assets, such as infographics, embedded videos, links to related websites, audiences, and linguistic structures. By incorporating students' assets, identities, and positionalities into our writing assessment, we center our students in the curriculum while also providing them with opportunities to engage in real-world writing that incorporates a range of literacy strategies and is written for authentic audiences.

How Can Asset-Based Writing Assessment Look in Action?

In this section, we'll describe three examples of asset-based writing assessments that Sean used with a ninth-grade English class. In each example, you'll find important information related to the assessment: a description of the product that the students created, a discussion of how the assessment related to students' assets, and a reflection on what the assessment can show us about asset-based writing assessment. We share this information to provide specific examples of what asset-based writing assessment can look like in one setting and to convey insights regarding how and why the assessments connect to students' assets. We feel all of this information works together to illustrate key components of asset-based writing assessment: it's important to look at examples of this concept to see how this assessment approach can look in action, but it's also essential to create assessments that align with the unique writing assets, attributes, and identities of your students. We encourage you to consider these assessments as models for how you can apply the idea of asset-based writing assessment in your classroom.

Assessment Example One: "Changing Minds" Podcast and Website
Product Students Created
In this project, each student created a podcast and an associated website dedicated to raising awareness of and changing others' minds about a topic, event,

or person. Because of the project's focus on raising awareness and changing minds, the students were encouraged to select a subject that they felt was frequently misunderstood or not fully understood by others. One of the ways the class prepared for this is by examining other texts (from a wide range of genres) that have the ability to change others' minds about important topics. Students read and reflected on excerpts from nonfiction books *The 57 Bus* (Slater, 2017) and *Alexander Hamilton* (Chernow, 2004) and articles from *Sports Illustrated* and *Teen Vogue*. In addition, students carefully analyzed Malcolm Gladwell's (2016–present) *Revisionist History* podcast, which describes itself on its website as

> a journey through the overlooked and the misunderstood. Every episode re-examines something from the past—an event, a person, an idea, even a song—and asks whether we got it right the first time. Because sometimes the past deserves a second chance.
>
> (para. 1)

Students listened to multiple Gladwell podcasts (some that Sean selected and some of their own choosing) and discussed and analyzed their content and approach. In addition, the students looked at the website for the *Revisionist History* podcast, focusing primarily on the specific pages on the website for each individual episode. In many cases, these pages introduce the audience to the content of that episode and provide sources and links to news articles, primary sources, and other information that gives the audience additional context for the topic.

After examining these texts, students began to identify topics that they felt might be misunderstood or not fully understood by at least some people and then researched them, finding and utilizing sources that provided important information about the topic that can illuminate others' understandings. Students used this research to write podcast scripts that introduced the topic, identified misunderstandings or examples of limited understanding, and provided information addressing this concept. In addition, students created websites associated with their podcast episodes informed by the *Revisionist History* site that introduced the topic of the podcast and shared links to a range of research and information about the podcast's focal concept.

How This Assessment Related to Students' Assets

This assessment connected to students' interests in and familiarity with podcasts: as discussed in Chapter 3, the students with whom Sean worked greatly enjoyed listening to a wide range of podcasts and recommending them to each other. Students often spoke highly of podcasts that provided in-depth information about topics, which is a key feature of the *Revisionist History* podcast series. In addition to the opportunity to create podcasts, this assessment also aligned with students' interests in multimedia in general: by creating a webpage that described their podcast and providing links to news articles, primary sources, and other research, the students could utilize multimedia in ways that support the podcast they created. By curating these sources, students were able to communicate information in multimedia-focused ways. In addition, the website they created resembled the supplementary materials that accompany some real-world podcasts.

Furthermore, this assessment related to students' interests in societal issues, providing them with the freedom and flexibility for students to engage with issues that are especially meaningful to them. When brainstorming for this project, students first thought about social issues and concepts that they found to be particularly significant. Then, they identified aspects of those issues about which they wanted to change peoples' minds. By approaching the content in this way, students were able to research an issue that mattered to them and do so in a way that provided direction and purpose to the research they did and the work they ultimately created. Working to change others' minds about these topics motivated the students because it allowed them to advocate for perspectives, ideas, and issues that were important to them. Since Sean's students not only liked to engage with social issues but also liked to try to convince others about the merits of their positions, this opportunity to change others' minds aligned with their assets perfectly!

What This Assessment Can Show Us About Asset-Based Writing Assessment

This assessment illustrates a way that teachers can use students' assets to help them engage with research. While asset-based writing opportunities can certainly align with personal writing and individual experiences (Fletcher & Portalupi, 2001), opportunities like the one described here show how we educators can use students' assets to help them conduct meaningful research that is done with authentic audiences and purposes in mind. When students are able to conduct research about topics that matter to them and convey the results of that research with real-world audiences, they are able to see research as meaningful, relevant, and connected to their interests. In addition to providing students with the opportunity to engage with high-interest topics and share findings with real-world audiences, this assessment also conveys that there are many ways to convey the results of research through modalities that align with students' assets. By writing the text of a podcast that they would then narrate, students were able to write for real-world contexts that they identified as especially relevant and meaningful. While this is one specific example of an asset-based writing assessment, its core components can be widely applied to other educational situations. When our students are able to research topics that matter to them, share their findings with authentic audiences, and convey their ideas through modalities that align with their interests, assets, and out-of-school lives, they can see research and writing as concepts with relevance and authenticity that can be shared through a range of modalities.

Assessment Example Two: Poems and Multimedia Presentations
Products Students Created

In this project, students created poems that they felt represented or described something that mattered to them, such as an issue, experience, or individual. In addition, the students constructed multimedia presentations that they felt aligned with their poems by representing similar themes, emotions, and topics. In these presentations, students selected photographs, artwork, memes, and short video clips that they felt aligned with their poems. The students then shared these poems and their corresponding multimedia presentations with their classmates and with other guests they invited to the event. To do so, students read their poems out loud while their multimedia presentations played behind them. The combination of the students' reading their works and the multimedia displays provided a multisensory experience for the audience and gave the students a variety of ways to convey key ideas that mattered to them. After the presentations, students then submitted their poems and the slides of their presentations—their grades were based on the poems they created, the multimedia in their presentations, and how the two worked together to create a cohesive experience that represented related, yet still distinct, information.

To prepare for their creation of this product, students thought carefully about how a written text can align with accompanying multimedia. In one activity, they worked in groups to select and analyze published poems by identifying key themes and concepts they addressed and then selected multimedia they felt aligned with ideas in those works. For example, one group analyzed the poem "Still I Rise" by Maya Angelou (1978) and selected a variety of historical and contemporary images that they felt represented the idea of overcoming obstacles and oppression. The students then gave presentations in which they shared the poems they used while playing the associated multimedia they identified. This gave the students experience doing what they would later do with their own poems by linking the concepts and ideas in a written text with multimedia images and short videos that represented similar messages. In addition, Sean modeled this work for students: he wrote a poem about issues of injustice, created a multimodal presentation consisting of photographs and artwork that he felt aligned with the message of the poem, and presented it to the class in the ways the students ultimately did. This modeling activity gave the students a concrete example of what this work can look like as they created their own pieces aligned with their interests.

How This Assessment Related to Students' Assets

This assessment used students' assets to help them engage with and create poetry. Using topics and modalities that resonated with the students, this assessment provided them with an accessible and engaging opportunity to work with a genre that a number of students in the class expressed previously having difficulty with and a lack of interest in. In this assessment, students were able to choose to utilize their insights into social issues, their personal experiences, and their feelings about individuals who impacted their lives. In addition, students were able to incorporate their interest with multimedia through their selection of photographs, artwork, memes, and video clips that align with the piece's key concept. Through these opportunities to engage with relevant issues and incorporate multimedia in meaningful ways, students were able to incorporate their assets in their work creating and thinking carefully about the key ideas in poetry. When provided with an assessment form that incorporated their assets in both content and modality, students eagerly worked with a genre that they had previously found intimidating: they embraced the asset-based opportunities to reflect on and write about meaningful topics and identify multimedia that corresponded with those concepts.

What This Assessment Can Show Us About Asset-Based Writing Assessment

This assessment shows one way that students' assets can be used to make accessible a genre that students previously found intimidating or challenging. In this project, students worked with, thought carefully about, created, and shared poetry while doing so in ways that incorporated their engagement with multimedia and their interests in social issues and other topics that they found relevant. While this is one example, its overarching ideas have a great deal of relevance to writing assessment in a larger context: by incorporating a wide range of students' assets in their assessments (and in the associated instruction that prepares students to create the products on which they're assessed), we can create writing experiences that draw on the skills our students bring to the classroom while still challenging them to learn about a variety of writing-related genres and concepts.

One especially noteworthy aspect of this assessment that can be applied to asset-based writing assessment in general is the range of students' assets it incorporated. This product not only drew on topics that interested students, but also made use of their familiarity and engagement with multimedia. Applied to a broader educational context, this assessment shows that students have so many assets that they can add into the writing-related products they create, such as topics, modalities, interests, community connections, and other forms of authentic applications. We can center our students and incorporate their assets in a variety of ways when creating opportunities for them to demonstrate their knowledge—if we create space for our students to incorporate their assets in their writing assessment products, we can work to construct equitable and meaningful spaces in which our students' unique attributes are incorporated and valued.

Assessment Example Three: Public-Service Announcement Videos
Product Students Created
In this project, students examined examples of public-service announcement videos, studied rhetorical strategies used in those videos and a range of other texts, and ultimately worked in groups to create their own public-service announcement videos about causes or issues that they identified as important. To create these videos, student groups constructed storyboards, wrote scripts and accompanying stage directions, acted, and recorded their public-service announcements. In preparation to do this work, students learned about and reflected on the rhetorical concepts of ethos, logos, and pathos, noting their presence in a variety of works, such as professionally made public-service announcement videos, print and online advertisements, and articles from newspapers, magazines, and websites. They then considered how to use these rhetorical appeals to maximize the effectiveness of their public-service announcement videos, discussing how to use a combination of these strategies to convince their audience of the importance of their message. In addition, students looked at published public-service announcement videos and examined them as mentor texts, noting the tactics that the videos use (such as strategies like close-ups, voiceovers, music, and graphics) to make the work as effective as possible. After creating these videos, the class then held a "film festival" for others in the school, guests, and community members interested in engaging with the works the students constructed. At the "film festival," each group gave a brief introduction to their video in which they discussed why they selected the topic they picked and what they learned from the experience.

How This Assessment Related to Students' Assets
This assessment incorporates the students' interests in social issues and multimedia, providing them with opportunities to advocate for topics that

matter to them and to use multimedia tools to engage in that advocacy. In addition to incorporating these important assets, this assessment provided students with opportunities to share their insights with authentic, real-world audiences: the "film festival" at the end of the project served as a way for students to share their works with audiences other than the teacher. This event was attended by a variety of individuals—teachers in the school brought their classes to watch and students invited family members, caregivers, and other community members. For example, a group of students who created a public service announcement about the importance of making youth sports affordable invited one of their baseball coaches from an out-of-school league, providing another example of an authentic audience for that work.

Another way that this assessment aligned with students' assets is the way the videos students created aligned with authentic language they use in their out-of-school lives. While sharing their perspectives on the topics addressed in their respective videos, students communicated their ideas and insights in language they would use in real-world, out-of-school contexts to convey the importance of this topic. One component of the assessment that facilitated this was the audience with which the works would be shared: since students knew that these works would be viewed at the "film festival" by a variety of individuals from their school and community, they indicated that they would use language that they would use with that audience. Another aspect of the project that promoted authentic language use was the type of interactions that took place in the videos themselves: the public-service announcement videos students created contained scenes in which the students interacted with each other in situations based on real-world scenarios. The language students used in these scenes corresponded with the ways they would authentically communicate in such a real-world context, such as interactions between peers focused on the benefits or cautions associated with a particular issue or activity. The connections between this assessment and real-world scenarios facilitated the use of authentic communication, which further incorporated students' assets through real-world language.

What This Assessment Can Show Us About Asset-Based Writing Assessment

This assessment shows the value of creating opportunities for students to apply academic concepts to real-world situations that align with their authentic interests. In this specific example, students demonstrated their knowledge of the rhetorical concepts of ethos, logos, and pathos through an assessment that was authentic and asset-based in a variety of ways: it provided them with opportunities to apply their knowledge to real-world issues, it allowed them to incorporate forms of multimedia, and it created ways for them to construct real-world situations through the scenarios in their public-service announcement videos. These components, while specific to this particular assessment, certainly have applicability to authentic and asset-based assessment in general: when we construct opportunities for our students to demonstrate knowledge, it is important that those opportunities are based on who our students are and provide them with meaningful applications of concepts and strategies they learn in school.

No matter the specific concepts or strategies our students learn, it's essential to provide assessment opportunities that align with real-world-oriented demonstrations of that knowledge. When we do this, we construct assessments (and learning environments) that create opportunities for our students to meaningfully incorporate their communities and lived experiences in the classroom. By doing so, we position ourselves in dialogue (Van Sluys, 2011) with our students by engaging with and learning about their out-of-school lives while guarding against deficit-oriented instructional and assessment approaches that harm students, especially those who have been negatively impacted by traditional assessments (New York University, 2020). When we create opportunities for students to employ and incorporate their assets in their writing assessments, our classrooms become student-centered places in which students are able to apply knowledge in meaningful ways. Whether your students are learning about the rhetorical strategies central to this assessment or any other writing concept, assessments that center their unique identities and provide them with authentic opportunities will maximize their success and engagement.

Key Ideas to Keep in Mind When Putting Asset-Based Writing Assessment Into Action

This section describes five key ideas to consider when implementing asset-based writing assessments with your students. The information shared here will help you enhance the impact and relevance of writing assessment by aligning it with your students' unique assets, attributes, and experiences. The five insights we recommend keeping in mind are:

- ◆ Reflect on your experiences with writing assessment.
- ◆ Consider how writing assessments can be made as inclusive as possible.
- ◆ Learn about your students' range of writing-related assets.
- ◆ Craft writing assessment opportunities for students that align with their writing-related assets.
- ◆ Continue to adapt writing assessments for students as they learn new content and you learn more about their assets, experiences, and interests.

Now, let's examine each of these insights individually.

Reflect on Your Experiences With Writing Assessment

As you work toward incorporating students' assets in their writing assessments, we recommend beginning the process by thinking about your experiences with writing assessment. Specifically, we suggest considering your writing-assessment-related experiences as both a student (especially in the grade or grades you currently teach) and as a teacher. Reflecting on these experiences, we believe, establishes a meaningful starting point for the growth in assessment-related knowledge that this process facilitates. For example, before Sean worked on crafting the asset-based writing instruction practices discussed in this chapter, he first thought about the writing assessment he experienced as a student: "There was a lot of focus on mechanics," he told himself. "I also remember a lot of emphasis on structure, such as where a thesis statement goes and how to organize a paragraph." After this, Sean thought about his work with writing assessment as a teacher: "I've done a lot with giving my students choices of topics," he reflected, "and that's gone really well. One thing I'd like to do more of is incorporating more genres into the writing assessments I give my students. I think this would help engage them and make their writing experiences more authentic."

Sean's ideas provide an example of what this process can look like; we recommend engaging in similar reflection to help you begin to think about writing assessment. To reflect on your experiences with writing assessment as a student, we suggest answering the following questions:

- ◆ What were some of the ways my writing was assessed?
- ◆ What was primarily emphasized on these assessments?
- ◆ What conclusions did I draw and what feelings did I have about writing based on these assessments?

In addition, we suggest thinking about the writing assessments you've used with your students and reflecting on what aspects of those assessments have most struck you as effective and meaningful. These questions can facilitate thoughtful analysis of your experiences assessing writing:

- ◆ What do I value when I assess writing?
- ◆ How do those values inform the writing assessments I use with my students?
- ◆ What writing assessments have seemed to motivate and engage my students?
- ◆ What else might I do to create engaging and meaningful writing assessments for my students?

These questions, which are also available in an easily reproducible format in Appendix B, represent an important step toward implementing asset-based writing assessments with your students. By thinking about your experiences as both a student and a teacher, you'll engage in important reflective work that will help you deepen your understanding of what writing assessment has been for you and what it can become.

Consider How Writing Assessments Can Be Made as Inclusive as Possible

After reflecting on your experiences with writing assessment, we recommend using those reflections and insights to think even further about issues of inclusivity in the ways writing is traditionally assessed. Your recollections and ideas about what writing assessment has looked like and what was emphasized in those assessments position you to think about limitations in writing assessments, such as the audiences, modalities, and topics that have traditionally been valued. As we've addressed in this book, traditional methods of literacy assessment not only limit our students' opportunities to succeed, but contribute to deficit thinking (New York University, 2020) by ignoring students' cultural knowledge and unique experiences (Gibson, 2020). There are a variety of ways that writing assessment can be done in inclusive ways, such as making space for multimedia (Stockman, 2020), creating space for translanguaging, in which multilingual students incorporate multiple languages in their works (Kabuto, 2019), constructing opportunities for students to write in their home languages, such as the linguistic forms in which they engage in their homes and communities (Gibson, 2020), and providing opportunities for students to share work with authentic audiences (Fletcher & Portalupi, 2001).

These insights into inclusive writing assessment provide an important framework to use when thinking about how we can construct assessment opportunities in our classrooms that center students and privilege their assets and experiences. As we'll continue to explore in these recommendations, the best writing assessments are those that are aligned with our individual students. However, an essential aspect of being able to connect writing assessment with students' assets is being aware of some of the forms that inclusive and student-centered writing instruction can take; this knowledge then sets us up to be able to incorporate these assessments into our classrooms in ways that align with who our students are. To facilitate this, we encourage you to brainstorm some possible ways that you can see yourself incorporating multimedia, translanguaging, students' home languages, and authentic audiences in writing assessment. Appendix B contains a reproducible document titled "Brainstorm: Inclusive Writing Assessment Practices" that you can use when considering ways that you might incorporate these practices in writing assessments.

Learn About Your Students' Range of Writing-Related Assets

An essential part of constructing asset-based writing assessments is listening to and learning from your students regarding their writing-related assets. While it's important to brainstorm general insights about inclusive writing assessments (as discussed in the previous recommendation), it's impossible to create writing assessments that align with our students' assets unless we first learn what those assets are. This involves decentering ourselves in the classroom (Stockman, 2020) and placing our students' identities, cultures, and experiences in a central role. As the examples in this chapter convey, students' assets can take a wide range of forms, such as multimodal expression, specific interests and topics, community connections, and authentic language.

When Sean began to learn about his students' assets, one of the first steps he took was asking students to share their thoughts on the types of content with which they like to engage, the content they like to create, the topics that interest them, audiences with which they have shared their ideas or would like to share their ideas, and the modalities they have used or would like to use to share their insights. The form Sean used to ask students to share this information is available in Appendix B in the document titled "Student Writing Asset Information Sheet." After your students share this information, we recommend reading the documents twice: first to get a general sense of your students' writing-related assets and interests and then a second time to identify key themes and ideas that emerge. For example, when Sean examined the forms his students completed, he initially read them to learn more about his students and get to know them better, identifying issues that matter to them and content with which they liked to engage, such as podcasts and YouTube videos. After that, he reflected on the ideas shared in these works more holistically, making note of the students' interests in social issues, multimodal compositions, and opportunities to share ideas with real-world audiences.

Craft Writing Assessment Opportunities for Students That Align With Their Writing-Related Assets

Once you've learned about your students' writing-related assets, you'll be well-positioned for the next step of this process: using students' assets to craft authentic assessment opportunities for students. As with the literature-related assets described in Chapter 3, it's likely that there will be some variation as well as some similarities in your students' writing-related assets, interests, and experiences. Because of this, we encourage you to construct writing assessments that incorporate common aspects of your students' assets while still providing individual students with the flexibility to align their work with their unique interests, identities, and positionalities. For example, in the writing-related assessments described in this chapter, Sean constructed opportunities for students to utilize their assets related to social issues, multimodal expression, authentic audiences, and authentic language while still making the assessments open-ended enough for students to have freedom in the specific topics they addressed and in some of the ways they brought their individual assets to the assessments. The poetry and multimedia presentations, for instance, were inspired by students' interests in multimedia and engagement in societal issues, but incorporated opportunities for students to draw on their unique perspectives and interests while constructing their works.

When constructing writing assessments you'll use with your students, we recommend considering what writing skills you want your students to demonstrate in the assessment, what students will do in the assessment, how the assessment will show you if students have demonstrated the identified skills, how the assessment corresponds with students' assets, and what opportunities for variation, differentiation, and student choice are present in the assessment. The document "Asset-Based Writing Assessment Planning Guide" in Appendix B will help you reflect on these issues; it asks you to comment on each of these topics for the assessment you're planning. By considering these issues and incorporating them into your writing assessments, you'll ensure that your students will have opportunities to demonstrate their writing knowledge in meaningful, asset-based ways that provide opportunities for their unique perspectives and insights.

Continue to Adapt Writing Assessments for Students as They Learn New Content and You Learn More About Their Assets, Experiences, and Interests

Asset-based writing assessment is an ever-evolving process for a variety of reasons. Not only do we learn more about our students' assets as we continue to teach them, but students also develop new interests, ideas, and experiences on which they can draw in authentic assessments. In addition, students will work with new genres and writing concepts throughout the academic year, which presents new and different opportunities to draw on their assets to help them engage with writing-related ideas and skills. While we certainly encourage you to use the resources in Appendix B and the ideas in this chapter to get to know your students' writing assets at the beginning of the year, we want to encourage you to see these ideas and documents as starting points for the journey of asset-based writing assessment. Seeing asset-based writing assessment as a continued and fluid process helps us as teachers grow in our assessments as we continue to engage with and learn about our students.

For example, when designing the multimedia and poetry presentations described in this chapter, Sean not only drew on his knowledge of the students' assets but also on their apprehension and difficulties with writing poetry; he used his awareness of the students' identities and of their academic experiences and reservations to construct poetry assessments that were student-centered, relevant, and engaging. In addition, when constructing the public-service announcement video assessments, Sean incorporated his students' assets as well as the writing concepts of ethos, logos, and pathos to provide them with an assessment experience that centered them while also incorporating essential writing strategies. As you implement asset-based writing assessment in your classroom, we encourage you to keep reflecting on your students' assets, noting new developments, and using those insights to provide them with meaningful assessments that align with the writing-related insights about which they're learning. We'd love to hear about the amazing work that takes place in your classroom!

5

Asset-Based Language Assessment—Using Inquiry and Authentic Application to Engage With Grammar, Vocabulary, and Language

In this chapter, we'll apply our asset-based approach to language assessment by looking closely at what it means to incorporate students' assets when assessing their grammar and vocabulary knowledge. First, we'll explore what asset-based language assessment is, examining key goals of language assessment and describing how these assessments can meaningfully incorporate students' assets. Next, we'll dive into why asset-based language assessment is particularly important, noting the benefits of language assessment practices that center students and identifying how practices that don't take students into account can be harmful and counterproductive. After that, we'll look closely at specific examples of asset-based language instruction that Sean used with his ninth graders, discussing what these assessments were, how they related to students' assets, and what they reveal about asset-based language assessment. Finally, we'll share key suggestions to consider as you work to implement asset-based language assessments in your work with your students. By implementing asset-based language assessments in our classrooms, we can help our students have authentic, meaningful, and culturally sustaining (Paris, 2012) experiences with this important aspect of literacy assessment.

DOI: 10.4324/9781003264934-8

What Is Asset-Based Language Assessment?

Language assessment, which we define here as the evaluation of students' understandings of grammar and vocabulary, has an important place in the conversation about asset-based assessment. While many traditional methods of grammar and language instruction emphasize activities that are disconnected from authentic applications and student writing (Wotjer, 1998; Ruday, 2020), there are a variety of ways to authentically incorporate and make connections to students' assets, cultures, and real-world experiences as they learn about and demonstrate their knowledge of grammatical and vocabulary-related concepts. Instead of assessment activities that focus primarily on out-of-context memorization recall, asset-based language assessments create opportunities for students to apply linguistic understandings to their unique funds of knowledge (Gonzalez, Moll, & Amanti, 2005) and positionalities.

To construct asset-based language assessments for students, it's important that we prioritize authentic application: students can demonstrate their knowledge of linguistic concepts in meaningful and relevant ways by looking for examples of those concepts in their out-of-school lives, reflecting on the impact of those concepts, and considering why that particular linguistic element was used in that situation. For example, when Sean worked with his ninth graders on authentic language study, he constructed opportunities for the students to look for grammar and vocabulary-related concepts in text forms that they found especially engaging, such as memes and song lyrics. In addition, he created space for students to look for these concepts when exploring topics that resonated with them, such as works related to their interests in social action and community issues. Through these assessment opportunities, students demonstrated their knowledge of grammatical concepts, word roots, and domain-specific vocabulary in relevant ways that corresponded with their assets and experiences.

Like we've discussed with asset-based literature and writing assessments in Chapters 3 and 4, respectively, the specific ways you make language instruction aligned with your students' assets will vary based on their identities and positionalities. One class, for example, might greatly enjoy looking for grammatical concepts and vocabulary elements in sports broadcasts, while students in another class might not engage with that topic. It's essential that we as teachers consider who our students are, what assets, experiences, and identities they bring to the classroom, and how they can draw on those features to demonstrate their knowledge in meaningful and relevant ways. As we'll explore in more depth in this chapter, these assessments center our students by placing their identities and assets in a central role in language instruction, thereby avoiding approaches that prioritize factual recall of academic concepts without any connection or relevance to students' lives (Duncan-Andrade & Morrell, 2005). Asset-based language instruction goes beyond worksheets and memorization to provide students with authentic opportunities to apply their knowledge of language and vocabulary.

Why Is Asset-Based Language Assessment Important?

Asset-based language assessment is essential to constructing a culturally relevant (Ladson-Billings, 1995) and culturally sustaining (Paris, 2012) classroom environment. This approach provides an important equitable contrast to deficit-based language ideologies (Lanehart, 2002), which are instruction and assessment practices that focus primarily on identifying what students do not know rather than using asset-based approaches that build on and incorporate what students do know (Gibson, 2020). Deficit-based and out-of-context approaches to language study not only can create negative feelings among students (Wotjer, 1998), but also can contribute to oppressive and exclusionary methods of instruction by only valuing limited perspectives and viewpoints. For instance, language assessment that privileges inflexible rules without opportunities for analysis, nuance, or authentic application can harm students by presenting them with limited perspectives on language use (Ruday, 2021). This is especially troublesome when we take into account that deficit-based language ideologies (Lanehart, 2002) and associated traditional forms of language instruction and assessment are "most typically associated with middle-class White speakers" (Woodard & Kline, 2016, p. 6) and are not inclusive of language varieties and authentic applications. Limited and deficit-based perspectives on language instruction and assessment can result in anti-Black linguistic racism (Baker-Bell, 2020) and other harmful effects on students.

To avoid the problems that stem from deficit-oriented language instruction, we need to change the way grammar and vocabulary is approached in the classroom. Instead of approaching grammar and vocabulary through a lens that emphasizes correcting students and asking them to demonstrate knowledge in prescribed, out-of-context ways, it's on us as teachers to think about how we can assess our students' knowledge in ways that value the language experiences and identities they bring to the classroom. If we do this, we can construct culturally sustaining (Paris, 2012) and inclusive opportunities for students to convey what they know about grammar and vocabulary and to demonstrate that knowledge in authentic ways. By taking an asset-based approach to language assessment, we can incorporate our students' funds of knowledge (Gonzalez, Moll, & Amanti, 2005) and positionalities in meaningful and engaging ways while working to construct inclusive learning environments. Instead of our students seeing language assessment as focused on compliance, memorization, and out-of-context activities, we can reconstruct this aspect of our assessment practice in relevant ways that center students' real-life experiences. In the next section, we'll check out some ways this approach can look in action.

How Can Asset-Based Language Instruction Look in Action?

Now that we've discussed key features of asset-based language assessment and considered why it's so important to students' inclusive English language arts experiences, let's look at some examples of how it can look in action. This section contains three descriptions of asset-based language assessments that Sean used with his ninth graders: each one discusses the product that the students created, how it related to students' assets, and what that activity can show us about asset-based language assessment. These descriptions will provide you with concrete examples of what asset-based language assessment can look like in one particular setting and how the features of those assessments aligned with students' assets in that context. As you read about these examples, we encourage you to think about how you might implement language assessments in your classroom that align with the unique identities and positionalities of your students. Sean implemented these language assessments with his students because of the ways these practices centered them and aligned with their assets; by examining these examples, you'll have concrete models from which you can draw as you construct asset-based language assessments with your students.

Assessment Example One: Grammar Inquiry Projects
Product Students Created
In this activity, titled The Grammar Inquiry Project (Ruday, 2020), students worked individually to select a grammatical concept they studied that year and to conduct an inquiry into ways that they saw that concept used authentically in texts they encountered outside of school. To conduct these inquiries, students identified examples of their selected concepts and analyzed the significance of those concepts to the effectiveness of the texts in which they were originally used. After engaging in this identification and analysis, students shared the results of their inquiries through multimedia presentations

they gave in a concluding celebration. In these presentations, students shared authentic examples of the grammatical concepts they identified, using relevant media to convey this information to the audience. For example, students who found examples of a focal grammatical concept in songs would play excerpts from those songs and identify the relevant concept. Similarly, students who noted them on social media posts would share those posts and identify the grammatical concept in the post. Some students identified examples of grammatical concepts in conversations with others, such as community members, sports teammates, or relatives: since they didn't have multimedia of the exact conversation, these students used images of the content in which the communication took place and/or the individuals in the conversation to help the audience further engage with and understand the situation in which the grammatical concept was used.

Sean and the students worked together through a four-step process to help them ultimately share their identifications and analyses of authentic grammatical concepts (Ruday, 2020). First, Sean talked with the students about the purposeful use of grammar, identifying a number of grammatical concepts the class had discussed earlier in the school year and discussing how those concepts are important to effective communication. For example, Sean highlighted the topic of prepositional phrases and shared a range of texts in which writers used that concept to provide important detail that was essential to understanding key ideas in the piece. After that, Sean introduced The Grammar Inquiry Project: to do this, he described the project, explained to students what product they would ultimately create, and modeled his own inquiry and analyses. When modeling an inquiry, Sean again highlighted the concept of prepositional phrases, sharing authentic examples of prepositional phrases that he found in texts he encountered in his everyday life. Since Sean is an avid sports fan, he shared examples of prepositional phrases in sports broadcasts he watched and articles he read. After that, he shared analyses of the importance of these prepositional phrases to the contexts in which they were used. Next, Sean conferred with students as they identified grammatical concepts in texts they encountered in their out-of-school lives and analyzed their importance. Finally, the students presented the results of their grammar inquiries to an audience of their classmates, other students and teachers in the school, their families and caregivers, and community members they chose to invite.

How This Assessment Related to Students' Assets

This assessment connected to students' assets by providing them with individualized opportunities to identify and think critically about grammatical concepts. Because the assessment called for students to examine texts they encounter in their out-of-school lives, it has a natural connection to students' authentic assets, interests, and experiences. When selecting and analyzing texts for this project, students were able to draw on a range of forms of communication and select examples that they felt to be personally relevant. During the introduction of this project, Sean emphasized the range of forms that texts can take in this context, noting that students could identify grammatical concepts in a wide variety of works, including (but not limited to) books, poems, song lyrics, social media posts, and community conversations. In addition, when modeling this project for the students, Sean purposefully selected sports broadcasts and articles for his identification and analysis of prepositional phrases to emphasize that the texts students used for this activity could take much more varied forms than those they encountered in school. Students took advantage of this opportunity to draw on a range of texts by analyzing topics related to their interests, such as social media posts about societal issues, songs they felt were relevant to the world today, YouTube broadcasts with which they engaged, and popular memes.

Another way that this assessment aligned with students' assets is the multimodal aspect of the students' presentations. By incorporating multimedia that either conveyed or related to the authentic uses of grammatical concepts the students identified and analyzed in their presentations, they were able to incorporate their expertise and interest in multimodal tools when sharing the results of their inquiries. These opportunities to incorporate multimedia had a number of important benefits: they further engaged students in their work, they drew on students' experiences, and they helped the students connect with the authentic audiences that came to see them share their insights. For example, if a student identified an example of a grammatical concept in a song and played the relevant excerpt from that song while displaying the lyrics that conveyed that concept, that student's work would represent all three of these important benefits: playing and displaying the lyrics would maximize the student's engagement, connect to their experiences, and provide content and presentation components that would help the audience engage with the work. The connections this assessment facilitated to students' multimodal assets maximized the relevance and effectiveness of their Grammar Inquiry Projects.

What This Assessment Can Show Us About Asset-Based Language Assessment

This project demonstrates that grammar assessment can incorporate students' authentic interactions with language and can do so in ways that promote in-depth analyses of and engagement with those concepts. Since out-of-context grammar instruction and assessment practices lead to student disengagement (Wotjer, 1998) and have very little impact on student writing (Weaver, 1998), it's clear that we educators need another way to teach and assess grammar in our classrooms. The Grammar Inquiry Project described here provides a model for what student-centered grammar assessment can look like; it illustrates that meaningful assessments of grammatical concepts can draw on students' funds of knowledge (Gonzalez, Moll, & Amanti, 2005), create space for our students' voices and perspectives (Lyiscott, 2019), and strategically center students while decentering teachers (Stockman, 2020).

As you incorporate asset-based grammar assessments in your classroom, we encourage you to draw on key components of the project described here. We strongly recommend providing students with meaningful opportunities to identify, analyze, and share how grammatical concepts are used in texts that are relevant to and authentically used in their out-of-school lives. When doing this, you'll certainly want to consider your students' unique assets, ideas, and experiences in your decision-making process in order to incorporate and center them in their learning assessment processes. Student-centered grammar assessments like The Grammar Inquiry Project illustrate the amount of agency that students can and should have in their work with language assessments. Instead of relying on memorization-based activities, worksheets, and other out-of-context methods, we can construct opportunities for students to draw on their assets and authentic literacy practices while demonstrating understandings in meaningful ways. Assessment methods like these lead to culturally sustaining (Paris, 2012) classrooms, which are possible when we center our students as they learn about and demonstrate their knowledge of academic concepts.

Assessment Example Two: Word Root Identifications and Analyses
Product Students Created
In this assessment, students applied their knowledge of Greek and Latin word roots by identifying examples of words that contained the word root of their choice (Ruday, 2018). To do the assignment, each student identified a word they encountered in their out-of-school life that contained one of the Greek or Latin word prefixes, bases, and suffixes they had been learning about in their English class. Figure 5.1 contains some of the word roots that Sean discussed with the students. (The chart depicted in Figure 5.1 is also available in reproducible form in Appendix B.)

Students then created and shared infographics that contained the following information: the word they identified, the context in which they encountered the word, the Greek or Latin word root it contains, the meaning of the root, the meaning of the word, and an explanation of how the word's meaning and the root's meaning align.

To guide students through this instructional and assessment process, Sean first conducted a series of mini-lessons about Greek and Latin word roots in which he talked with students about the importance of those concepts

Root	Meaning
Anti	Against
Arch	Most important
Bio	Life
Celer	Fast
Cert	Sure
Dem, Demo	People
Extra, Extro	Beyond
Geo	Related to the earth
Mal	Bad, wrongful
Max	Largest
Mem	Mind
Omni	All
Path	Emotion
Post	After
Sol	Sun
Un	Opposite
Ver	Truth

Figure 5.1 Greek and Latin Root Examples

to language study, their prevalence in the English language, and the ways that understanding these roots can help them learn vocabulary. Next, Sean shared a variety of words that contain the roots the class had examined, noting that those words can be used in a wide variety of contexts and situations, explaining:

> As you learn about and pay attention to these word roots, it's likely that you'll encounter them in a whole bunch of situations. For example, just yesterday, I heard the prefix 'post' in a lot of different contexts. In a class, a student asked a question about postmodern literature. Then, I read on social media that an event I was planning to attend had been postponed. Later that evening, I watching a basketball game on television and the announcers referred to the postgame show. So, that's three uses in different settings of the word root 'post.'

After discussing these examples with the students, Sean shared with them the details of the assignment on which they would demonstrate their knowledge of Greek and Latin roots, describing the infographics they would create and share for this assessment and what information those infographics would contain. To help students understand the details of this assessment, Sean modeled what the product students would create would look like, sharing an example of an infographic he created. In Sean's infographic, he focused on the word "archrival," which he heard being discussed in a sports broadcast that featured two professional hockey teams, the Pittsburgh Penguins and Philadelphia Flyers. In accordance with the assignment, Sean's infographic also identified the prefix "arch" contained in the word, its meaning ("most important"), and his explanation of how the word's meaning aligns with the root's. Sean explained to his students,

> The word root 'arch' means 'most important,' and the announcers on the hockey game I was watching referred the Penguins and Flyers as 'archrivals,' which means 'most important or most significant rival.' These two teams really want to beat each other for a few reasons: they play in the same state, they're both good teams, and their fans care a lot about this game. These factors are part of the reason they're archrivals.

After describing the assignment and modeling this example, Sean spent the next several classes supporting students as they identified and analyzed authentic examples of Greek and Latin roots used in words they encountered in their out-of-school lives. Once the students completed their identifications, analyses, and corresponding infographics, they shared their insights with the other students in the class, the other ninth-grade English classes in the school, and guests they invited by displaying and describing their infographics.

How This Assessment Related to Students' Assets

This assessment related to students' assets by centering students' authentic interactions with language, providing them with real-world applications of the language-related concepts of Greek and Latin word roots. As with the previously described Grammar Inquiry Project, the opportunity for students to identify and analyze linguistic concepts in their out-of-school lives provided the assessment with built-in authenticity and applicability. By asking students to note situations in which they found examples of Greek and Latin roots in texts with which they engaged outside of school, this assessment was designed to be asset-based and authentic. In addition to helping students apply their knowledge of Greek and Latin word roots, this assessment sought to incorporate relevance and engagement (Duncan-Andrade & Morrell, 2005) into vocabulary instruction by privileging students' funds of knowledge (Gonzalez, Moll, & Amanti, 2005). As Sean demonstrated in the hockey-based examples he modeled for students, this assessment provided students with opportunities to incorporate and draw on their unique interests and experiences when identifying and analyzing examples of Greek and Latin roots in authentic texts.

In addition, this assessment aligned with students' assets through its incorporation of multimedia-based infographics and the opportunities it provided for students to share their insights with authentic audiences. In their infographics, students not only documented their insights related to Greek and Latin roots, but also incorporated multimedia and other visuals that aligned with the context of the words they identified. For example, a student who identified an example of a word root in a popular song used images of the singer, graphics of musical notes, and a font and color scheme similar to one the singer used on an album cover to align the details of the infographic with the featured musical artist. Since the students in this class were particularly engaged with multimedia, the opportunity to incorporate images, graphics, colors, and other details in their infographics helped them individualize their works in ways that aligned with their assets. Also, this project drew on the students' interest in sharing their ideas with others by incorporating an authentic audience to which they would convey their infographics and associated insights. By presenting their findings and infographics to their classmates, other students in the school, and guests they invited, students were able to convey to an authentic audience the out-of-school examples of word roots they identified and the multimedia-related choices they made when constructing their infographics.

What This Assessment Can Show Us About Asset-Based Language Assessment

This assessment illustrates the power and impact of asset-based language assessment by demonstrating that these assessments can be authentic, engaging, and academically rewarding. It was not only engaging and relevant to students, but also required students to think in complex and analytical terms about the Greek and Latin word roots they studied. A key takeaway from this assessment is that effective vocabulary assessment can center students through authentic opportunities for them to make connections to their out-of-school lives. This framework can be applied to other forms of language instruction and assessment: as we teach our students about linguistic concepts (such as the word roots discussed here), we can maximize the effectiveness of our instruction and assessment by constructing opportunities for students to apply their knowledge in real-world situations. Through these authentic connections, students can see that the linguistic concepts they learn about in school are not only present in school, but rather are used in a range of contexts, such as in texts the students encounter outside of school. By developing this awareness, students can maximize their abilities to make sense of the world around them while also learning concepts that will help them succeed in school. Assessments such as this can help our students enhance their language skills in authentic ways while merging school and community and collapsing separations that exist between the two (Tremmel, 2006).

Assessment Example Three: Connotation and Denotation in Social Media Posts

Product Students Created

In this project, students identified connotation-rich language they used in social media posts, replaced the relevant words with words that had the same denotation but different connotations, and analyzed the differences. After engaging in this identification, replacement, and analysis, students presented their findings to the class. In these presentations, each student shared a social media post they had previously created that they felt used language with a specific connotation. Then, they identified the connotation-rich language in the post and discussed its connotation and denotation. After that, they shared a new version of the text of the post that contained language with a similar denotation but different connotation and described the connotation of the new language. Finally, students concluded their presentations with their thoughts on how the two texts were different, the impact of the connotation of the original language on the post, and any closing insights they had about the importance of understanding connotation.

To prepare students to complete this assessment, Sean first talked with students about the concept of connotation, discussing its meaning and the difference between connotation and denotation. After that, the class looked together at a number of texts that contained connotation-rich language, examining examples from published books, song lyrics, social media posts, advertisements, television, and film. As the students looked closely at these examples, Sean helped them to see why it's so important to think carefully about the connotations of words we use and why this concept is an important component of effective communication. Following these conversations, Sean introduced the assessment project they would complete regarding connotations in social media posts, discussing the details and expectations described in the previous paragraph. Once students understood the products they would be creating, Sean worked with them individually on their connotation-related insights and analyses to help them prepare for the presentations they would give.

How This Assessment Related to Students' Assets

This assessment provided students with an authentic, applicable, and asset-based opportunity to consider the concept of connotation and its importance to effective communication. While the students certainly benefited from examining a wide range of connotation-rich mentor texts and examples, the assessment's focus on social media maximized its applicability and relevance. During the first two projects described in this chapter, Sean came up with the idea of connecting this assessment to social media—as students applied their knowledge of grammatical concepts and word roots in those projects, he noticed how carefully and thoughtfully they discussed the language they encountered and used on social media. Motivated by this asset that students demonstrated, he decided to align it with the topic of connotation that he knew the students were expected to study. By making connections to the language they used on social media, students were able to look at authentic uses of connotation-rich words and carefully reflect on their importance.

When presenting their findings to the class, students were further able to convey their insights on connotation with many of the same individuals who had previously encountered their social media posts. By talking about the impact and importance of the connotation-rich language they used on social media with authentic audiences of their peers who used the same or similar platforms, students had the opportunity to engage with a community with similar points of references and experiences. This further increased the applicability and authenticity of the project—if the students only shared their insights with the teacher instead of an audience of peers with similar experiences, the assessment may not have felt as meaningful or motivational for students. In this assessment, the audience of peers aligned with the authenticity of the work.

What This Assessment Can Show Us About Asset-Based Language Assessment

One important aspect of this assessment that has relevance to other classroom contexts is the way it conveys the wide range of possibilities of asset-based language instruction and assessment. While this is one example of an assessment in which students looked for authentic examples of a linguistic strategy, its takeaway ideas extend beyond one particular instance. The specific components of this assessment, such as the concept of connotation and the authentic text of students' social media posts, are certainly important to this particular project. However, this same framework can also be applied to a range of other assessments designed to provide students with authentic ways to convey their knowledge of a particular language concept. For instance, if we educators wanted to evaluate students' understandings of sensory imagery in writing, we could construct an assessment opportunity in which students look for authentic uses of sensory language, reflect on the importance of that language, and share their insights. The details can vary based on context, but the key framework of this assessment approach can be applied to a range of authentic uses of language and students' corresponding insights.

Another important takeaway from this assessment is that it further represents the significance of continuously learning about our students and their assets. By listening to the students' insights about the language they use when crafting social media, Sean learned about this asset his students possessed, which led him to design an assessment opportunity that incorporated this authentic application. The best asset-based language instruction and assessment, we feel, takes into account that students' linguistic assets have the potential to develop and to reveal themselves over time. Not only do we feel that it's likely that the kinds of texts and language uses in which students engage at the beginning of the school year will gradually change and shift throughout it, but we also believe that students have assets that teachers will understand through active listening to the students and engagement with them. In this way, asset-based language assessment leads to even more asset-based language assessment: by giving our students opportunities to demonstrate their knowledge in authentic ways, we learn more about what texts are authentic to our students and are then able to create additional assessment opportunities that incorporate our students' assets.

Key Ideas to Keep in Mind When Putting Asset-Based Language Assessment Into Action

Now, let's take a look at some essential recommendations to consider when putting asset-based language assessment into practice in your classroom. These insights are designed to help you structure your language assessments in meaningful, student-centered, and purposefully organized ways. The five suggestions we recommend keeping in mind are:

- ◆ Consider the benefits of asset-based language assessment.
- ◆ Learn about how your students authentically engage with language.
- ◆ Construct authentic opportunities for students to apply their knowledge of language.
- ◆ Support students as they apply linguistic concepts in asset-based and authentic ways.
- ◆ Continue to learn about your students' language assets and make adjustments according to your developing understandings.

Let's examine each of these recommendations individually.

Consider the Benefits of Asset-Based Language Assessment

To begin the process of designing asset-based language assessment, we encourage you to take a few minutes and think about the benefits of this practice. Before Sean began constructing language assessments for his students that centered them, their assets, and their unique funds of knowledge (Gonzalez, Moll, & Amanti, 2005), he spent some time thinking about the potential benefits of this practice, such as how it can engage students, ways it facilitates in-depth analysis of key grammar and vocabulary-related concepts, and the opportunities it provides for students to authentically demonstrate their knowledge. Sean felt that doing this was beneficial for a variety of reasons: for example, it helped him think carefully about how this assessment approach would center his students in their learning and encouraged him to reflect on his experiences with the memorization-based grammar and vocabulary assessments he experienced as a student, including how those practices emphasized recall of content without providing opportunities for authentic applications.

By considering these topics, Sean was able to identify and analyze the ways that asset-based language assessment can facilitate student learning. In addition, through this careful reflection, he was able to describe and justify this practice to anyone who had questions about it or wanted to know more. After Sean shared his thoughts and insights on asset-based language assessment with other teachers who asked him about it, many of these colleagues adopted similar practices, thereby helping their students have similarly relevant and engaging learning experiences. We encourage you to think about the benefits that you believe can come from asset-based language assessment and why you believe those benefits are present. Once you've done this, we recommend recording those observations on the document in Appendix B titled "Benefits of Asset-Based Language Assessment." By considering these ideas, you'll ensure that you've thought carefully about the positive effects of this practice and will be well positioned to share your insights with others.

Learn About How Your Students Authentically Engage With Language

An essential step toward implementing asset-based language assessment is learning about the ways your students authentically engage with language. This knowledge is essential to constructing assessments (and corresponding instructional practices) that align with our students' linguistic assets, experiences, and identities. By learning about the situations in which our students authentically interact with grammar and vocabulary-related concepts outside of school, we can then position ourselves to incorporate those real-world connections in their in-school work. One way that we recommend learning about your students' authentic language experiences is through an initial survey. When Sean began the work described in this book with his ninth graders, he asked them the following open-ended questions about the ways they encounter language outside of school:

- When you're not in school, what are some situations in which you communicate? Try to be as specific as you can. (These situations can be in-person or virtual and can take place in any context, such as in-person conversations with friends and family, social media inter-actions, text messages, interactions while playing sports or video games, or anything else that's relevant to you.)
- When you're not in school, what are some ways you encounter language without communicating directly with others? Again, try to be as specific as you can. (These are situations in which you read or listen to language but don't speak to other people directly, such as books and articles you read, material that you listen to—like music or podcasts, videos you watch—such as YouTube, television shows, movies, or anything else that aligns with your experiences.)

These questions are also available in reproducible form in Appendix B in the document "Student Language Asset Survey." By asking our students about their experiences with language, we create a situation in which we can learn about their authentic linguistic assets and then incorporate this information in the language instruction and assessment that takes place in our classrooms.

In addition to these using survey questions, we recommend carefully listening to your students as they discuss authentic contexts in which they communicate and encounter language. Through these informal observa-tions, you'll learn even more information than students may share on their surveys. While Sean certainly drew on his students' survey responses, he also made notes about what else his students shared as they discussed their authentic language experiences. When recording this information, Sean identified examples of out-of-school language contexts that his students described in class discussions, informal conversations, or on other assign-ments. For instance, a number of students noted that frequent communica-tion settings for them were conversations with family members and sports teammates. In addition, they noted that they frequently interacted with peers through social media. Some students also shared that while play-ing video games, they spoke to others verbally through their headsets and also communicated through online chat programs at the same time. The students also shared situations in which they encountered language with-out directly interacting with others: some high-frequency situations were music, YouTube videos, podcasts, and memes. The document "Observa-tions of Students' Language Assets" in Appendix B provides a reproduc-ible form that you can use to record what you notice about your students' language assets.

Construct Authentic Opportunities for Students to Apply Their Knowledge of Language

Now that you've carefully and thoughtfully learned about the situations in which your students engage with language in their out-of-school lives, it's time to construct authentic and asset-based assessment opportunities in which our students demonstrate their understandings of linguistic concepts. To construct these assessments, we recommend first reflecting on what you noticed about your students' language-related assets. To do this, you can look back on the information you collected in the previous step, identifying key information and important themes in the surveys your students completed and in the information that you noticed. By thinking carefully about this important information, you'll enhance your understanding of your students' linguistic assets. You'll draw heavily on these insights as you construct asset-based assessment opportunities for your students.

As you reflect on the details of your students' surveys and your insights, you'll also want to think about the linguistic concepts that you want your students to understand: this will represent the material on which students will demonstrate their knowledge as they complete their assessments. For example, in the language assessments described in this chapter that Sean crafted for his ninth graders, the first assessment focused on grammatical concepts the class studied up to that point in the school year, the second addressed Greek and Latin word roots, and the third evaluated students' knowledge of connotation. Once you've identified these focal concepts, the next step is to merge students' linguistic assets with these academic topics by crafting assessments that center students' unique experiences, identities, and interests. When you do this, one of the most important points to consider is the significance of creating opportunities for your students to apply their knowledge of language in ways that are authentic to them. The examples in this chapter provide models on which you can certainly draw when creating these assessments for your students, but it's essential that your assessments align with your particular students' assets and experiences by providing them with meaningful ways to apply their knowledge. The chart depicted in Figure 5.2 will guide you as you reflect on students' assets, the linguistic concepts on which you're focusing, and assessment opportunities that merge those assets and concepts. A reproducible version of this chart is also available in Appendix B.

Support Students as They Apply Linguistic Concepts in Asset-Based and Authentic Ways

Once you've created opportunities for students to demonstrate their language knowledge in asset-based ways, the next step is to support students as they work on these assessment products. Two key practices that can help

Students' assets	Linguistic concepts	Assessment opportunities that merge assets and concepts

Figure 5.2 Language Assessment Planning Chart

support students as they do this are modeling the kind of authentic application that students will do when they create their assessments and conferring with them individually as they work. Sean utilized each of these strategies when working with his ninth graders as they completed the language assessment described in this chapter and found each of them to make important impacts on his students' feelings of comfort and confidence with the assessment. Modeling the assignments provided students with clear expectations of the types of products they would create and gave Sean a natural opportunity to think aloud about the choices he made when constructing the product that he shared. In addition, sharing his asset-based assessment products allowed Sean to share information with the students about his authentic literacy practices, which showed students more about him as an individual and helped create a strong classroom community.

Conferring with students is a much different practice than modeling asset-based assessments for them, but Sean's students greatly benefitted from this practice as well. As students worked on identifying examples of linguistic strategies they encountered in authentic situations and analyzing their importance, Sean met with them individually to monitor their progress and provide them with individualized support. Sean talked with the students about the examples they identified and offered needed clarification if students needed additional guidance as they found examples of the focal concept or strategy. Once students moved to the analysis stage, Sean talked with them about what they had noticed about the significance of the examples they identified and asked probing questions to help guide their thinking and encourage their analyses. We strongly encourage you to utilize these individual conferences to support your students as they identify and analyze linguistic concepts used in authentic settings. The chart "Language Assessment Conference Guide," available in reproducible form in Appendix B, is designed to help you as you confer with your students. It asks you to note your observations about what your students have identified, the analyses they've created, strengths they've exhibited, areas of growth you've found, and what you focused on in your conversation.

Continue to Learn About Your Students' Language Assets and Make Adjustments According to Your Developing Understandings

As we've discussed throughout this section of the book, it's essential to understand that students' assets are continuously developing entities that will grow and adapt as they have new experiences, interact with their environments in different ways, and explore new cultural affiliations and affinity groups (Machado, 2017). We feel that this continuous development is especially relevant to asset-based language instruction: the authentic contexts in which students communicate and the ways they engage with language through texts they consume can adapt as they explore new interests, identities, and assets. Even when students' interests stay consistent, they will likely experience new texts and have new linguistic experiences as they continue to engage with the topics that matter to them.

There are multiple tactics you can use to continuously learn about students' developing language-related assets. One useful and easy-to-implement strategy is to note what types of texts and linguistic situations they incorporate in their assessments early in the school year; then, as you continue to create assessment opportunities for students, you can provide opportunities for students to make connections to these kinds of texts. For example, when constructing the third assessment described in this chapter, Sean decided to incorporate social media into the project after he noticed how the students reflected carefully and analytically about social media use when they completed the first two assessment projects. In addition, you can continue to use the informal observations discussed earlier in this chapter throughout the school year to learn about and make note of your students' developing language assets and experiences. By carefully observing and listening to your students as they share ways they authentically communicate and the real-world contexts in which they engage with language, you can continue to learn about their linguistic assets. We encourage you to use the document in Appendix B titled "Observations of Students' Language Assets" repeatedly throughout the school year to continually note your developing awareness of your students' language-related assets and experiences.

Part III
Putting It Together

6

How to Make a Case for Asset-Based Literacy Assessment

Having provided an introduction to what and why you might want to use asset-based assessment in your English class in the first two chapters and a glimpse into Sean's work with students who engaged in asset-based assessments in the last three chapters, we are now going to help you make a case to yourself and other stakeholders (e.g., students, parents, administrators, etc.) for the value of asset-based literacy assessment.

If you are thinking of trying out asset-based literacy assessment in your classroom, you will hopefully find this chapter to be a helpful resource to help you articulate to yourself why you want to give this assessment practice a try, share with colleagues why this practice may help your grade level team or department, and (and we hope this is not the case) defend your choice to various stakeholders (e.g., students, parents, and administrators).

Asset-based literacy assessment may align well with differentiated instruction. We acknowledge that differentiating instruction can be a challenging aspect of our work, and we think that asset-based literacy assessments can help. Our English classrooms include students who have different literature, writing, and language proficiencies; abilities; identities; previous experiences; motivations; and future goals. Asset-based literacy assessments can help you allow students to participate in the English curriculum in ways that work for them. In Chapter 3, Sean reveals how he used students' interests to engage them in literature study and projects that worked for them. Sharing with students and parents that you are offering students opportunities to meet literacy standards in ways that work for them can go a long way in terms of student engagement and motivation!

DOI: 10.4324/9781003264934-10

Asset-based literacy assessment privileges in-the-moment student growth in a way standardized testing does not. Just because asset-based assessment practices may look dissimilar to timed standardized tests, it does not mean that asset-based assessment practices cannot be pivotal to helping students meet particular content standards. Because these assessments are completed in a way in which teachers and students can work together in the context of an academic year, teachers can move students in particular areas and advance students' thinking about particular literature, writing, or language areas. We are not saying that standardized tests do not have any value, but they certainly do not allow learning in the moment in the way asset-based literacy assessments do. Asset-based literacy assessments permit students and teachers to work on addressing gaps in knowledge and accentuating areas of strength while keeping the focus on student growth. And we definitely do not think you would find many who would argue with your pedagogical practices if you and your students work on areas of need while showcasing assets as you document learning growth!

Asset-based literacy assessment practices prepare students for real-world, interdisciplinary projects. Although we as English teachers are intrinsically motivated to read fabulous texts or spend our leisure time writing pieces, we also understand that many of our students are not planning to be English teachers. And this is okay. Our world needs many different types of thinkers, and we believe that asset-based literacy assessments help prepare students for the types of professional and vocational workplaces in which they will find themselves after they leave our classrooms. Articulating that your asset-based literacy assessment practices is preparing students for the 21st century may be particularly convincing for students, parents, and administrators. The NCTE Framework for 21st Century Curriculum and Assessment (NCTE, 2013) shares that "active, successful participants in this 21st century global society must be able to:

- Develop proficiency and fluency with the tools of technology;
- Build intentional cross-cultural connections and relationships with others so as to pose and solve problems collaboratively and strengthen independent thought;
- Design and share information for global communities to meet a variety of purposes;
- Manage, analyze, and synthesize multiple streams of simultaneous information;
- Create, critique, analyze, and evaluate multimedia texts;
- Attend to the ethical responsibilities required by these complex environments" (para. 3).

When we think back to the units Sean shared in the previous chapters, we see that indeed many of the tasks students were doing were helping them build these skills. For example, when students created podcasts and websites about a misunderstood topic, they were working with technology tools, designing and sharing information for myriad purposes, and examining many streams of information. Helping students build the skills they will need to participate successfully in the world in which they find themselves when they move from our classrooms is indeed a major advantage for asset-based literacy assessment.

Asset-based literacy assessment practices may help you address challenges illuminated acutely in the past few years. None of us were ready for teaching through COVID. We realized certain aspects about teaching and learning during this time of remote teaching, teaching with masks, and ever-changing school schedules. Katie started her foundations of education course a few years ago with two rules for teaching: be flexible and wear comfortable shoes. No time in her teaching career did the first suggestion ring more true than in the past two years of teaching! And we're almost sure you feel the exact same way.

In 2020, the International Literacy Association published a literacy leadership brief titled "Meeting the COVID-19 Challenges to Literacy Instruction: A Focus on Equity-Centered Strategies." The brief highlighted several challenges that were illuminated in the last few years: digital access, transitioning to teaching and learning remotely, engaging anxious or disinterested students, focus on culturally responsive teaching, and inequitable opportunities to promote student and family relationships. Opportunities abound for asset-based literacy assessment to address these areas. These types of assessments can engage students who are anxious or disinterested because students can engage in projects with which they are connected. Similarly, culturally responsive teaching can be accomplished through these assessment practices because students are encouraged to engage in projects that align with their interests and identities. Relatedly, families can be involved in the assessments in which students engage in ways that make sense. The individualized nature of these assessments also makes them work when remote teaching is necessary because of illness or weather closures. And whereas we think students and teachers deserve a snow day here and there, our point is that students can work on these projects if schools have to make a pivot to remote learning.

Asset-based literacy assessment may reinvigorate your passion for teaching. There are not many of us who wanted to become an English teacher because we enjoy giving quizzes or administering standardized tests. We know the past few years have been particularly challenging for teachers, and the current context has not made the profession immune to attrition (NCTE,

2021). The pressures of preparing students for standardized tests and accounting for students' experiences in the past two years in addition to the personal health, family, and financial hardships many teachers have experienced has perhaps dulled some of your spark for teaching. Our hope, however, is that allowing yourself and your students to engage in the meaningful, authentic practices afforded by asset-based literacy assessments may rejuvenate your English classroom. Having opportunities to truly connect with your students in ways that are meaningful to them and offering students on-the-spot feedback in the context of students' projects may be just what you need to reinvigorate your passion for teaching.

Conclusion

As you consider incorporating asset-based literacy assessment into your English classroom, our hope is that this chapter has provided you some ways to articulate for yourself and others your pedagogical choice. We now transition to our key recommendations for using asset-based literacy assessment.

7

Key Recommendations for Implementation

Think back for a moment to the anecdote that begins this book: as Sean drove home one afternoon after working with his ninth graders, he reflected on the concept of assessment, noting the problems with a deficit-based assessment model and the benefits of asset-based assessments that provide authentic opportunities for students to apply knowledge in ways that facilitate connections to their experiences, identities, and cultures. After supporting his students as they created the asset-based assessment products described in this book, Sean thought further about the importance of this approach to assessment. One evening, while taking a walk outside, he reflected on what this experience showed him: "When I started thinking about asset-based assessment," he said to himself, "I had some initial thoughts about how these authentic and student-centered assessments can help students. Now," he continued, "after doing this and reflecting on it, I really understand how much asset-based assessments can transform education."

As Sean continued to think about the impact of asset-based assessments, he thought back to the range of authentic assessments his students completed and the ways those works conveyed their knowledge of literature, writing, and language in nuanced and in-depth ways. "These assessments motivated the students and honored their unique identities," he noted. "In addition, I believe they also resulted in much more in-depth analysis and critical thinking than deficit-based assessments would have." By drawing on their assets, experiences, and unique identities while demonstrating their knowledge, Sean thought, his students applied their understandings in authentic and meaningful ways that aligned with higher-order thinking and

DOI: 10.4324/9781003264934-11

deep understandings. "They thought about important academic content and applied it to the world around them," Sean said. "They did culturally relevant (Ladson-Billings, 1995) and culturally sustaining (Paris, 2012) work. Plus," he remarked, "the students were the ones who drove their assessment work— they applied the concepts in ways that were meaningful to them and were aligned with their assets."

These reflections on the benefits of asset-based assessment provide context for considering key recommendations to consider when implementing these assessment practices. By considering the suggestions presented in this chapter, you'll be well positioned to thoughtfully and purposefully implement asset-based literacy assessment in your work with your students. We recommend keeping these recommendations in mind as you think about, create, and utilize asset-based assessment:

◆ Reflect on issues of equity in assessment.
◆ Learn about your students' assets.
◆ Identify your curricular goals.
◆ Craft opportunities for students to demonstrate their knowledge in asset-based ways.
◆ Support your students through their work on asset-based assessments.
◆ Continuously reflect on what you've learned from your students' asset-based assessments and make adjustments accordingly.

In this chapter, we'll look at each of these recommendations individually, identifying and reflecting on key components of each one, what it looks like in practice, and why it's important.

Recommendation One: Reflect on Issues of Equity in Assessment

Before you begin to design asset-based assessment opportunities for your students, we urge you to take some time and think about the concept of equity and its relationship to assessment. As Sean began to work with his ninth graders on the assessments and corresponding instructional practices described in this book, he devoted time to reflecting on each of these issues. To do so, Sean did a free-write on each of these terms: he wrote about what came to his mind when he thought about equity in education and then what he associated with the concept of assessment. While reflecting on issues of equity in education, he listed the following topics as especially important: culturally relevant teaching (Ladson-Billings, 1995), culturally sustaining teaching (Paris, 2012), centering students, decentering teachers, student ownership, books that represent windows, mirrors, and sliding glass doors for students (Bishop, 1990), and authentic applications. When thinking about assessment, Sean's responses focused on what assessment was like for him as a student, the kinds of assessments he has used in his teaching career, and the kinds of assessments he would like to use as he continues to teach. In these reflections, Sean noted how much the assessments he experienced as a student were deficit-based and the ways he has worked to move away from this assessment approach and toward one that centers students and provides them with opportunities for ownership and application. "I need to continue to do this and to do even more of it with my students," Sean wrote, "because assessment that centers students creates equitable opportunities for students to succeed." Finally, Sean reflected in even more developed ways about the connection between equity and assessment, noting

> To have more equitable schools and educational experiences for our students, we need to really think about what assessment looks like. We need to move away from deficit-based approaches to assessment and create assessment for students that center them and draw on their assets.

We encourage you to engage in similar reflective practices as an initial step of your journey toward incorporating asset-based assessments in your classroom. Doing this will help you approach this process from a well-thought-out and introspective place by incorporating your insights and experiences regarding the concepts of equity and assessment. Through these reflections, you'll be able to think about what educational equity means to you, what you have noticed and experienced regarding literacy assessment, and how these two components intersect. The document "Equity and Assessment Reflection Guide" in Appendix B provides a framework that you can use as you engage in this reflection; modeled on the way Sean considered these topics, it contains spaces for you to free-write on equity in education and assessment, as well as space to record your thoughts on how these concepts connect. By engaging in these reflections, you'll activate your prior knowledge on these concepts and will ensure that you've thought carefully about these issues before constructing asset-based assessments.

Recommendation Two: Learn About Your Students' Assets

In order to incorporate asset-based literacy assessments in our classrooms, it's essential that we as teachers commit to learning about our students' assets.

Doing so provides us with essential understandings of students' identities, cultures, interests, and experiences; this knowledge is essential to creating authentic and meaningful opportunities for students to demonstrate their understandings in ways that center their assets instead of their deficits. As you learn about your students' assets, we recommend keeping these three suggestions in mind:

1. Find out about your students' assets early in the year through initial surveys and responses.

   An important first step toward learning about your students' assets is creating surveys and response questions that will help you know more about them. These can be questions about topics such as students' interests, events and issues (in their communities and in society in general) that matter to them, the texts they engage with outside of school, the ways they enjoy communicating, and their preferred tools of communication. These questions will not only help you learn about your students, but will also communicate to them your interest in what matters to them, which will help create a student-centered environment in your classroom. This book contains some examples of surveys and response questions you can utilize with your students; we encourage you to use these examples as starting points, but also to adapt them to incorporate any other specific information you'd like to know about your students. Through these adaptations, you can incorporate specific issues and topics that might be especially relevant to your students' interests, lives, and communities; this information will be useful as you create assessment opportunities that align with your students' assets and authentic experiences.

2. Listen to and observe your students to learn more about their assets, interests, and identities.

   In addition to using surveys and response questions to learn about students, we strongly recommend listening to and observing your students to find out about their assets, interests, identities, and experiences. When doing the work discussed in this book, Sean found that he learned a great deal of information and that helped him make his instruction asset-based and culturally sustaining (Paris, 2012) by talking with his students, listening to them discuss topics that matter to them, and noticing the funds of knowledge (Gonzalez, Moll, & Amanti, 2005), modalities, and texts that are authentic to who they are and what they value. As you identify this information, we encourage you to make note of each asset you feel your students possess and the ways they've demonstrated that asset. You can then read and reflect on these notes to further your understandings of your students and to incorporate this information in the assessments you create.

3. Continue to learn about your students' assets throughout the school year.

   The process of learning about our students' assets is fluid and ongoing: as we work with our students throughout the school year, it's essential that we continuously identify, reflect on, and act on information related to their identities, assets, and interests. While we should definitely learn about our students' assets early in the school year through surveys, reflection questions, observations, and conversations, it's also important to note that, for us to truly gain strong understandings of our students' assets, we need to think about this topic in continued and dynamic ways. We can do this by continually learning from our conversations with them, the work they do on their assessments, and ideas they share in their written and oral responses.

   One reason that it's essential for us teachers to notice and reflect on our students' assets throughout the school year is that the initial information we collect likely doesn't completely capture our students' identities; even if student surveys and teacher observations reveal a number of important topics that illustrate key aspects of our students, it's still very possible that there is more about our students for us to learn. Another reason is that our individual students' identities, interests, experiences, and assets may develop throughout the year. By consistently learning about our students, we can treat our students as the ever-changing and developing individuals they are instead of as static entities with fixed assets.

Recommendation Three: Identify Your Curricular Goals

An essential aspect of creating asset-based literacy assessments (and the corresponding instruction that prepares students for those assessments) is identifying the key academic concepts that you want your students to master. Although asset-based assessment is designed to center our students by incorporating their unique identities, positionalities, and experiences, these assessment practices are at their most meaningful when they center students in ways that provide them with opportunities to demonstrate their understandings of curricular concepts and learning objects. This alignment between assessment practices that center students and clear academic objectives corresponds with Ladson-Billings (1995) statement that culturally relevant pedagogy should help students achieve academic success while also incorporating and valuing their cultures. When constructing asset-based assessment opportunities for your students, we encourage you to select a skill, strategy, or concept on which you want to evaluate your students' knowledge. After you identify this information, you'll be well positioned to think about how to design assessments that provide students with ways to draw on their authentic interests, identities, and experiences while demonstrating knowledge of this topic. When designing the assessments described in this book, Sean thought carefully about the concepts and material he wanted to be sure his students understood. For instance, when crafting the language assessments detailed in Chapter 5, he thought about the grammatical concepts, Greek and Latin word roots, and the topics of connotation and denotation; after identifying this information, Sean felt ready to think about ways for students to demonstrate their knowledge in authentic and meaningful ways.

Recommendation Four: Craft Opportunities for Students to Demonstrate Their Knowledge in Asset-Based Ways

Now that you've identified the academic targets for your students to reach, you're ready to put your understandings of these curricular goals and your students' assets into action by creating student-centered assessment opportunities. As you do so, it's essential to think about how much an effective asset-based assessment is aligned with a particular educational context. In addition to the academic goals that you want your students to achieve, this context includes the issues and topics that matter to your students, their authentic, out-of-school literacy practices, the types of texts they like to create, the kinds of texts they consume, and the ways they communicate in their everyday lives. All of these attributes combine to create the literacy context present in your classroom. When constructing the assessments discussed in this text, Sean took all of these components into account in order to create opportunities for his students to demonstrate their knowledge in meaningful and student-centered ways. For instance, the asset-based literature assessments discussed in Chapter 3 drew on not only the texts students read, but also connected to their interests in social justice, goal-setting, community issues, and multimodal texts. By incorporating these student assets, Sean created individualized assessment opportunities that were unique to the context in which he was teaching.

It's important to note that assessments and instructional practices that correspond with the features of one context do not necessarily align with another. For example, the next time Sean works with students on Nic Stone's (2017) novel *Dear Martin*, he won't plan to use the same assessment that he did with the students in the class discussed in this book. Instead, he'll think carefully about the particular assets and interests of the students in that class and design assessments that align with those features. With this in mind, we encourage you to view the examples described in this book as models of asset-based assessment that are associated with a particular context. While it's possible that aspects of these assessments may align with other contexts, the most important component of effective asset-based assessments is that those assessments are informed by the specific instructional contexts for which they are created.

Recommendation Five: Support Your Students Through Their Work on Asset-Based Assessments

Asset-based assessments center our students and can greatly engage them in their academic work by drawing on their identities, experiences, and authentic literacy practices. However, this doesn't mean that we can simply give students an engaging assignment and just leave them to their own devices. Instead, it's essential that we teachers support and guide our students in ways that facilitate their understandings and successes as they work on these assessment projects. With this in mind, we've identified four ways to help students as they construct asset-based assessments:

1. Support students as they master the academic concept.
   In order for our students to successfully complete asset-based assessment products, they need to first understand the academic topic on which they're being assessed. Because of this, one of the key ways we can help our students do outstanding work on these assessments is by supporting them as they develop strong understandings of the concepts they're studying. Whether these concepts relate to key events and characters in a text that students have read, writing strategies and genres they're studying, grammatical concepts, word roots, or any other content they're learning, we can help our students succeed on their asset-based assessments by ensuring their understandings of this material. Once students have developed strong foundations related to these academic topics, they can

demonstrate their knowledge in meaningful, relevant, and asset-based ways.

2. Model the assessment for the students.

Before students work on asset-based assessment products, we recommend modeling your own work on it by creating an example of what that assessment can look like. When modeling this assessment work for your students, we encourage you to draw on your identity, experiences, and assets and to explain to students what you're doing and why you're doing so. For example, before his students worked on the language assessments discussed in Chapter 5, Sean shared examples of these assessments that represented his assets (such as the authentic use of the word root "arch" he noticed when watching a hockey game). As he presented students with this model, Sean explained that the example he was sharing was based on his interests and authentic experiences and that they would be drawing on their own unique identities when creating their assessment products. This modeling activity can provide students with clear understandings of the assignment while also building a strong classroom community that encourages authenticity and vulnerability.

3. Individually confer with students as they work on their assessment products.

Another especially important aspect of supporting students during their work on asset-based assessments is to hold one-on-one conferences with them while they complete these products. While the individual attributes of each conference will vary based on the particulars of the assessment students are constructing and the individual strengths and needs of each student, we recommend using the conferences to support students as they work to understand the focal academic associated with the assessment and as they apply those concepts in authentic ways. For example, when conferring with students as they created the public-service announcement videos described in Chapter 4, Sean supported their understandings of the rhetorical concepts of ethos, logos, and pathos, reviewing any necessary content, and then worked with them as they planned their videos, ensuring that they applied these topics to the products they created. It's essential to emphasize that these conferences are at their most effective when they revolve around students' needs, strengths, and attributes; by centering our students' unique understandings and characteristics in these conferences, we can maximize the success and usefulness of these meetings.

Step Six: Continuously Reflect on What You've Learned From Your Students' Asset-Based Assessments and Make Adjustments Accordingly

Finally, we encourage you to continue to reflect on the process of asset-based assessment throughout the school year. Earlier in this chapter, we pointed out the significance of continuing to learn about your students' assets as you work with them. In addition, after each assessment, it's important to think about what that experience showed you about your students, such as their identities, understandings, and assets and how you can use that information to shape your future asset-based assessments. We recommend taking some time after students complete each assessment to think about how they engaged with the format, navigated the level of choice the project provided to them, and used the assessment to convey their authentic ideas, interests, and funds of knowledge (Gonzalez, Moll, & Amanti, 2005). In addition, we suggest noting what the assessment revealed about students' academic strengths and areas of need. This knowledge will help you construct asset-based assessment opportunities that align with and are responsive to students' attributes in ways that align with their identities with respect to modalities, interests, cultures, and academics. By considering all of these topics, you'll engage in the continued reflection that will help you create effective asset-based assessments for your students.

Final Thoughts

Throughout this book, you've read about a number of different literacy assessments that incorporate students' assets and authentic interests. We are thrilled that you're thinking about ways to reject deficit-based assessment practices and to use assessments that honor students' assets and identities. Doing this is an essential step toward creating an inclusive classroom that values students' cultures and centers them in their learning. We'd like to close with an important concept to keep in mind when constructing asset-based opportunities for our students to demonstrate their knowledge: our students have rich ideas, perspectives, and experiences; the most effective assessments (and corresponding instructional activities) create opportunities for students to draw on those assets and use them to convey their understandings in meaningful and authentic ways. We're so happy that you've chosen to use this book to help guide you as you center your students in their assessment opportunities. Please reach out to us if we can help you as you do so!

Appendix A
A Guide for Book Studies

Sean and I always find it helpful to engage in professional book studies. There are face-to-face and online book studies with hundreds or a handful of colleagues. There is agreeing with a colleague in your building to read the same book and then meet for coffee or a walk to discuss. And then there is setting a personal goal to improve one's knowledge about a particular topic and setting out to read a book to do so.

In this appendix, we want to provide you with a guide to help you engage with, reflect on, and discuss the chapters in the book. Below you will find questions catered to each of the several chapters in the book. You can examine the questions as you progress through the book or wait until you have finished the book in order to examine these questions.

So brew up a cup of coffee or tea, and start reflecting and discussing!

Part I: Key Background and Context

Introduction: Time to Reimagine Literacy Assessment

1. Sean shares how he thought about assessment on his ride home one afternoon. What thoughts about assessment do you have on your ride home?
2. In what ways do you engage or hope to engage your students' interests with your assessment practices?
3. What reflections on assessment practices in your English classroom have you been having?

4. What may be the affordances of asset-based assessment practices?
5. What are your goals for reading this book on asset-based assessment practices?

Chapter 1: Key Principles of Asset-Based Literacy Assessment

1. When you first think of *assessment*, what comes to mind? What about *asset*?
2. In what ways were you taught or not taught to assess students in your English classroom?
3. How do you currently assess students? How are students a part of these decisions?
4. How do you envision using assessment practices that are centered on what students know?
5. How do you use or envision using assessment practices that are student centered?
6. What are the affordances and challenges of the ways in which asset-based assessment is discussed in Chapter 1?
7. What questions do you have as you move toward Chapter 2?

Chapter 2: Why Should We Adopt an Asset-Based Approach to Literacy Assessment?

1. What are some reasons why you are considering adopting an asset-based approach to literacy assessment?
2. What are some of the affordances of an asset-based approach to literacy assessment shared in the chapter?
3. With which affordance shared in the chapter do you most align? Why?
4. Which affordance shared in this chapter do you think most aligns with your students? Why?

Part II: Asset-Based Literacy Assessment Practices

Chapter 3: Asset-Based Literature Assessment—Moving Away From Quizzes and Toward Authentic Engagement With Relevant Issues

1. What comes to mind when you hear the phrase *literature assessment*?
2. In what ways (if any) have your literature assessment practices evolved as you have progressed in your teaching career?
3. How have you or how can you incorporate students into your literature assessment practices?

4. What were your biggest takeaways from the practices shared in this chapter?
5. What are your goals for asset-based literature assessment after reading this chapter?

Chapter Four: Asset-Based Writing Assessment—Exploring Societal Change, Multimodal Expression, and Linguistic Dive

1. What comes to mind when you hear the phrase *writing assessment*?
2. In what ways (if any) have your writing assessment practices evolved as you have progressed in your teaching career?
3. How have you or how can you incorporate students into your writing assessment practices?
4. What were your biggest takeaways from the practices shared in this chapter?
5. What are your goals for asset-based writing assessment after reading this chapter?

Chapter Five: Asset-Based Language Assessment—Using Inquiry and Authentic Application to Engage With Grammar, Vocabulary, and Language

1. What comes to mind when you hear the phrase *grammar, vocabulary, and language assessment*?
2. In what ways (if any) have your grammar and vocabulary assessment practices evolved as you have progressed in your teaching career?
3. How have you or how can you incorporate students into your language assessment practices?
4. What are your biggest takeaways from the practices shared in this chapter?
5. What are your goals for asset-based grammar, vocabulary, and language assessment after reading this chapter?

Part III: Putting It Together

Chapter Six: How to Make a Case for Asset-Based Literacy Assessment

1. What cases are made for using asset-based literacy assessment?
2. Which case for using asset-based literacy assessment do you find most convincing?

Chapter Seven: Key Recommendations for Implementation

1. We asked you to think about your views about assessment at the beginning of the book. How have your views about assessment changed now that you have finished the book?

2. How can you apply the six goals to keep in mind as you think about, create, and utilize asset-based assessment in your English classroom?

3. What goals do you have for yourself in the three areas of asset-based literacy assessment shared in this book: asset-based literature instruction, asset-based writing instruction, and asset-based language instruction?

Appendix B

Reproducible Forms and Templates

This section contains easily reproducible forms and templates designed to guide you as you put the ideas described in this book into action in your classroom. We encourage you to use these forms as you reflect on and plan for asset-based assessment practices that you will utilize to make your assessments as meaningful, student-centered, and asset-based as possible.

Reflection Questions on Literature Assessment Experiences

These reflection questions, described in Chapter 3, are designed to guide you as you think about your experiences with literature assessment—both as a student and as a teacher.

Reflection Questions on Your Experiences as a Student
- How was my knowledge of literature typically assessed?
- What do I remember about these assessments?
- What did I do when I prepared for these assessments?

Reflection Questions on Your Experiences as a Teacher
- What are some ways I have assessed my students' knowledge of literature?
- Which literature assessments seem to have best motivated my students to learn and express their knowledge?
- Why do I think those assessments were especially effective?

Notes on Students' Assets

You can use the document to identify assets you've noticed in your students and how they've displayed them. These assets can be family and community funds of knowledge (Gonzalez, Moll, & Amanti, 2005), interests, experiences, forms of technology in which students frequently communicate, modalities with which they engage, or other attributes. While this document lists space for four assets, you can certainly use this form multiple times to identify more.

◆ **Asset:**
  ◆ Ways students have displayed this asset:

◆ **Asset:**
  ◆ Ways students have displayed this asset:

◆ **Asset:**
  ◆ Ways students have displayed this asset:

◆ **Asset:**
  ◆ Ways students have displayed this asset:

Asset-Based Literature Assessment Planning Guide

We recommend using this graphic organizer to plan for asset-based literature assessment. This planning guide asks you to identify the student asset that is central to the assessment, the literary text or texts on which students are demonstrating their knowledge, what students will be asked to do in the assessment, how the assessment aligns with students' assets, and how it will allow students to display their knowledge of the text. While the main purpose of this guide is to help you plan for the assessment, it is also a useful way to convey the benefits of this assessment approach to others who may have questions about it.

Student asset that is central to the assessment	Text(s) on which students are demonstrating knowledge	What students will do in this assessment	How the assessment aligns with students' assets	How the assessment will allow students to display their knowledge of the text

Reflection Questions on Writing Assessment Experiences

These reflection questions, described in Chapter 4, are designed to help you think about your experiences with writing assessment as a student and as a teacher. By reflecting on these ideas, you'll take an important step in the process of thinking about asset-based writing assessment.

Reflection Questions on Your Experiences as a Student
◆ What were some of the ways my writing was assessed?
◆ What was primarily emphasized on these assessments?
◆ What conclusions did I draw and what feelings did I have about writing based on these assessments?

Reflection Questions on Your Experiences as a Teacher
◆ What do I value when I assess writing?
◆ How do those values inform the writing assessments I use with my students?

- What writing assessments have seemed to motivate and engage my students?
- What else might I do to create engaging and meaningful writing assessments for my students?

Brainstorm: Inclusive Writing Assessment Practices

Inclusive writing assessments can involve the purposeful inclusion of multimedia tools (such as infographics, podcasts, and videos), translanguaging (in which multilingual students incorporate multiple languages in their works) (Kabuto, 2019), opportunities for students to write in their home languages (such as the linguistic forms in which they engage in their homes and communities) (Gibson, 2020), and opportunities for students to share work with authentic audiences (Fletcher & Portalupi, 2001). We encourage you to use this chart to brainstorm some ways you can see yourself incorporating multimedia, translanguaging, students' home languages, and authentic audiences in writing assessment.

Concept:	Multimedia	Translanguaging	Students' home languages	Authentic audiences
How you might incorporate it in writing assessment:				

Student Writing Asset Information Sheet

When Sean began to learn about his students' writing assets, he used this form to learn more about the types of content with which they like to engage, the content they like to create, the topics that interest them, audiences with which they have shared their ideas or would like to share their ideas, and the modalities they have used or would like to use to share their insights. We recommend using this survey to find out some initial information about your students' writing-related assets, interests, and experiences.

What are some examples of content (related to any genre, modality, or topic) with which you like to engage? (It can be something you read, view, listen to, or anything else and can be related to any platform.)

What are some examples of content (again, related to any genre, modality, topic, or platform) that you like to create?

What are some topics about which you have enjoyed creating content or about which you would like to create content?

What are some modalities you have enjoyed using or which you would like to use when creating content?

Asset-Based Writing Assessment Planning Guide

We recommend using this graphic organizer to plan for asset-based writing assessment. This planning guide asks you to identify what writing skills you want your students to demonstrate in the assessment, what students will do in the assessment, how the assessment will show you if students have demonstrated the identified skills, how the assessment corresponds with students' assets, and what opportunities for variation, differentiation, and student choice are present in the assessment. While the main purpose of this guide is to help you plan for writing assessment, it is also a useful way to convey the benefits of this assessment approach to others who may have questions about it.

Writing skills you want your students to demonstrate	What students will do in this assessment	How the assessment will show you if students have demonstrated the identified skills	How the assessment corresponds with students' assets	What opportunities for variation, differentiation, and student choice are present in the assessment

Figure 5.1 Greek and Latin Root Examples

This chart features some of the Greek and Latin roots Sean discussed with his students as he prepared them to identify words containing Greek and Latin roots that they encountered in their out-of-school lives.

Root	Meaning
Anti	Against
Arch	Most important
Bio	Life
Celer	Fast
Cert	Sure
Dem, Demo	People
Extra, Extro	Beyond
Geo	Related to the earth
Mal	Bad, wrongful
Max	Largest
Mem	Mind
Omni	All
Path	Emotion
Post	After
Sol	Sun
Un	Opposite
Ver	Truth

Benefits of Asset-Based Language Assessment

An important initial step of incorporating asset-based language assessment in your classroom is reflecting on the benefits of this practice. Before Sean began constructing language assessments for his students that centered them, their assets, and their unique funds of knowledge (Gonzalez, Moll, & Amanti, 2005), he spent some time thinking about the potential benefits of this practice, such as how it can engage students, ways it facilitates in-depth analysis of key grammar and vocabulary-related concepts, and the opportunities it provides for students to authentically demonstrate their knowledge. We encourage you to use this resource to identify some benefits that you feel are present in asset-based language assessment and why you believe those benefits are present.

Benefit you feel comes from asset-based language assessment	Why you believe that benefit is present in asset-based language assessment

Student Language Asset Survey

By learning about the situations in which our students authentically inter-act with grammar and vocabulary-related concepts outside of school, we can then position ourselves to incorporate those real-world connections in their in-school work. One way that we recommend learning about your students' authentic language experiences is through an initial survey. When Sean began the work described in this book with his ninth graders, he asked them the following open-ended questions about the ways they encounter language outside of school:

◆ When you're not in school, what are some situations in which you communicate? Try to be as specific as you can. (These situations can be in-person or virtual and can take place in any context, such as in-person conversations with friends and family, social media inter-actions, text messages, interactions while playing sports or video games, or anything else that's relevant to you.)

◆ When you're not in school, what are some ways you encounter language without communicating directly with others? Again, try to be as specific as you can. (These are situations in which you read or listen to language but don't speak to other people directly, such as books and articles you read, material that you listen to—like music or podcasts, videos you watch—such as YouTube, television shows, movies, or anything else that aligns with your experiences.)

Observations of Students' Language Assets

We also recommend carefully listening to your students as they discuss authentic contexts in which they communicate and encounter language. Through these informal observations, you'll learn even more information about your students' linguistic assets. You can use this document to record what you notice about the contexts your students describe.

Context	How students have expressed communicating and/or encountering language in this context

Language Assessment Planning Chart

This chart will guide you as you reflect on students' assets, the linguistic concepts on which you're focusing, and assessment opportunities that merge those assets and concepts.

Students' assets	Linguistic concepts	Assessment opportunities that merge assets and concepts

Language Assessment Conference Guide

This chart is designed to help you as you confer with your students while they create asset-based language assessments. It asks you to note your observations about what your students have identified, the analyses they've created, strengths they've exhibited, areas of growth you've found, and what you focused on in your conversation.

Student name_____

Conference date_____

The linguistic strategy the student identified	The student's analysis of the strategy	Strengths exhibited	Areas of future growth	Focus of conference conversation

Equity and Assessment Reflection Guide

The document provides a framework that you can use as you reflect on equity and assessment; it contains spaces for you to free-write on equity in education and assessment, as well as space to record your thoughts on how these concepts connect.

What you think about when you reflect on equity in education:

What you think about when you reflect on assessment:

How you feel the concepts of equity in education and assessment connect:

References

Angelou, M. (1978). *Still I rise.* www.poetryfoundation.org/poems/46446/still-i-rise

Association of College and Research Libraries. (2018). *5 things you should read about asset-based teaching.* ACRL. https://acrl.ala.org/IS/wp-content/uploads/is-research_5Things_asset-based-teaching.pdf

Atwell, N. (2015). *In the middle: A lifetime of learning about writing, reading, and adolescents.* Portsmouth, NH: Heinemann.

Baker-Bell, A. (2020). *Linguistic justice: Black language, literacy, identity, and pedagogy.* New York, NY: Routledge.

Bishop, R.S. (1990). Mirrors, windows, and sliding glass doors. *Perspectives: Choosing and Using Books for the Classroom, 6*(3), ix–xi.

Brown, D.F., & Knowles, T. (2014). *What every middle school teacher should know.* Portsmouth, NH: Heinemann.

Burke, J. (2013). *The English teachers' companion.* Portsmouth, NH: Heinemann.

Cartaya, P. (2017). *The epic fail of Arturo Zamora.* New York, NY: Puffin Books.

CAST. (2018). *Universal design for learning guidelines version 2.2.* http://udlguidelines.cast.org

Chernow, R. (2004). *Alexander Hamilton.* New York, NY: Penguin Books.

Dueck, M. (2021). *Giving students a say: Smarter assessment practices to empower and engage.* Alexandria, VA: ASCD.

Duncan-Andrade, J., & Morrell, E. (2005). Turn up that radio, teacher: Popular cultural pedagogy in new century urban schools. *Journal of School Leadership, 15*(3), 284–304.

Fletcher, R., & Portalupi, J. (2001). *Writing workshop: The essential guide.* Portsmouth, NH: Heinemann.

Gibson, V. (2020, February 26). *Working toward culturally responsive assessment practices.* National Council of Teachers of English Blog. https://ncte.org/blog/2020/02/working-toward-culturally-responsive-assessment-practices

Gladwell, M. (Host). (2016–present). *Revisionist history* [Audio podcast]. Pushkin Industries. https://www.pushkin.fm/show/revisionist-history/

Gonzalez, N., Moll, L.C., & Amanti, C. (2005). Introduction. In Gonzalez, N., Moll, L.C., & Amanti, C. (Eds.) *Funds of knowledge: Theorizing practices in households, communities, and classrooms.* New York, NY: Routledge.

Hall, L. (2010). *Empowering struggling readers: Practices for the middle grades*. New York, NY: Guilford.

Hammond, Z. (2015). *Culturally responsive teaching & the brain*. Thousand Oaks, CA: Corwin.

International Literacy Association. (2020). *Meeting the COVID-19 challenges to literacy instruction: A focus on equity-centered strategies*. www.literacy worldwide.org/docs/default-source/where-we-stand/ila-meeting-the-COVID-19-challenges.pdf

Kabuto, B. (2019). *Assessing linguistically diverse students*. National Council of Teachers of English Blog. https://ncte.org/blog/2019/10/assessing-linguistically-diverse-students/

Ladson-Billings, G. (1995). But that's just good teaching! The case for culturally relevant pedagogy. *Theory into Practice, 34*(3), 159–165.

Lanehart, S.L. (2002). *Sista, speak!: Black women kinfolk talk about language and literacy*. Austin, TX: University of Texas Press.

Lyiscott, J. (2019). *Black appetite. White food*. New York, NY: Routledge Eye on Education.

Machado, E. (2017). *Culturally sustaining pedagogy in the literacy classroom*. International Literacy Association Literacy Now Blog. www.literacy-worldwide.org/blog/literacy-now/2017/05/31/culturally-sustaining-pedagogy-in-the-literacy-classroom

Milner, J.O., Milner, L., & Mitchell, J.F. (2012). *Bridging English*, 5th ed. New York, NY: Pearson.

Mirra, N. (2018). *Educating for empathy*. New York, NY: Teachers College Press.

National Council of Teachers of English. (2013). *NCTE framework for 21st century curriculum and assessment (positions and guidelines)*. https://cdn.ncte.org/nctefiles/resources/positions/framework_21stcent_curr_assessment.pdf

National Council of Teachers of English. (2018). *Literacy assessment: Definitions, principles, and practices* [Position Statement]. https://ncte.org/statement/assessmentframingst/

National Council of Teachers of English. (2020). *Expanding formative assessment for equity and agency* [Position Statement]. https://ncte.org/statement/expanding-formative-assessment/

National Council of Teachers of English. (2021). *Recognizing teacher experts and their paths to expertise* [Position Statement]. https://ncte.org/statement/recognizing-teacher-experts-and-their-paths-to-expertise/

New York University Steinhardt School of Education. (2020, September 16). *An asset-based approach to education: What it is and why it matters*. Teacher Education Reinvented. https://teachereducation.steinhardt.nyu.edu/an-asset-based-approach-to-education-what-it-is-and-why-it-matters/#:~:text=%E2%80%9CAsset-based%20teaching%20seeks%20to,highlights%20students'%20inadequacies.%E2%80%9D%20

Paris, D. (2012). Culturally sustaining pedagogy: A needed change in stance, terminology, and practice. *Educational Researcher, 41*(3), 93–97.

Pew Research Center. (2019). *Most U.S. teens see anxiety and depression as a major problem among their peers.* www.pewresearch.org/social-trends/2019/02/20/most-u-s-teens-see-anxiety-and-depression-as-a-major-problem-among-their-peers/

Robb, L. (2010). *Teaching middle school writers: What every English teacher needs to know.* Portsmouth, NH: Heinemann.

Ruday, S. (2018). *Culturally relevant teaching in the English language arts classroom: A guide for teachers.* New York, NY: Routledge Eye on Education.

Ruday, S. (2020). Grammar, ownership, and usefulness: Student-centered inquiries into authentic uses of grammatical concepts through The Grammar Inquiry Project. *Virginia English Journal, 69*(2), 22–28.

Ruday, S. (2021). Anti-oppressive grammar instruction: A call to action for educators. *ATEG Journal, 30*(1), 9–17.

Slater, D. (2017). *The 57 bus.* New York, NY: Farrar, Straus and Giroux.

Stephens, J. (2017). *Cultivating a culturally responsive classroom community.* Scholastic EDU. https://edublog.scholastic.com/post/cultivating-culturally-responsive-classroom-community

Stockman, A. (2020). *Creating inclusive writing environments in the K-12 classroom.* New York, NY: Routledge Eye on Education.

Stone, N. (2017). *Dear Martin.* New York, NY: Ember.

Thomas, A. (2017). *The hate u give.* New York, NY: HarperCollins.

Tremmel, R. (2006). Changing the way we think in English education: A conversation in the universal barbershop. *English Education, 39*(1), 10–45.

Van Sluys, K. (2011). *Becoming writers in the elementary classroom: Visions and decisions.* Urbana, IL: NCTE.

Watson, R. (2017). *Piecing me together.* New York, NY: Bloomsbury.

Weaver, C. (1998). Teaching grammar in the context of writing. In Weaver, C. (Ed.) *Lessons to share on teaching grammar in context* (pp. 18–38). Portsmouth, NH: Boynton, Cook.

Wiliam, D. (2013). Assessment: The bridge between teaching and learning. *Voices from the Middle, 21*(2), 15–20.

Woodard, R., & Kline, S. (2016). Lessons from sociocultural writing research for implementing the common core state standards. *The Reading Teacher, 70*(2), 207–216.

Woodard, R., Vaughn, A., & Machado, E. (2017). Exploring culturally sustaining writing pedagogy in urban classrooms. *Literacy Research: Theory, Method, and Practice, 66*, 215–231.

Wotjer, S. (1998). Facilitating the use of description-and grammar. In Weaver, C. (Ed.) *Lessons to share on teaching grammar in context* (pp. 95–99). Portsmouth, NH: Boynton, Cook.

For Product Safety Concerns and Information please contact our EU
representative GPSR@taylorandfrancis.com
Taylor & Francis Verlag GmbH, Kaufingerstraße 24, 80331 München, Germany

www.ingramcontent.com/pod-product-compliance
Ingram Content Group UK Ltd.
Pitfield, Milton Keynes, MK11 3LW, UK
UKHW031041080625
459435UK00013B/575